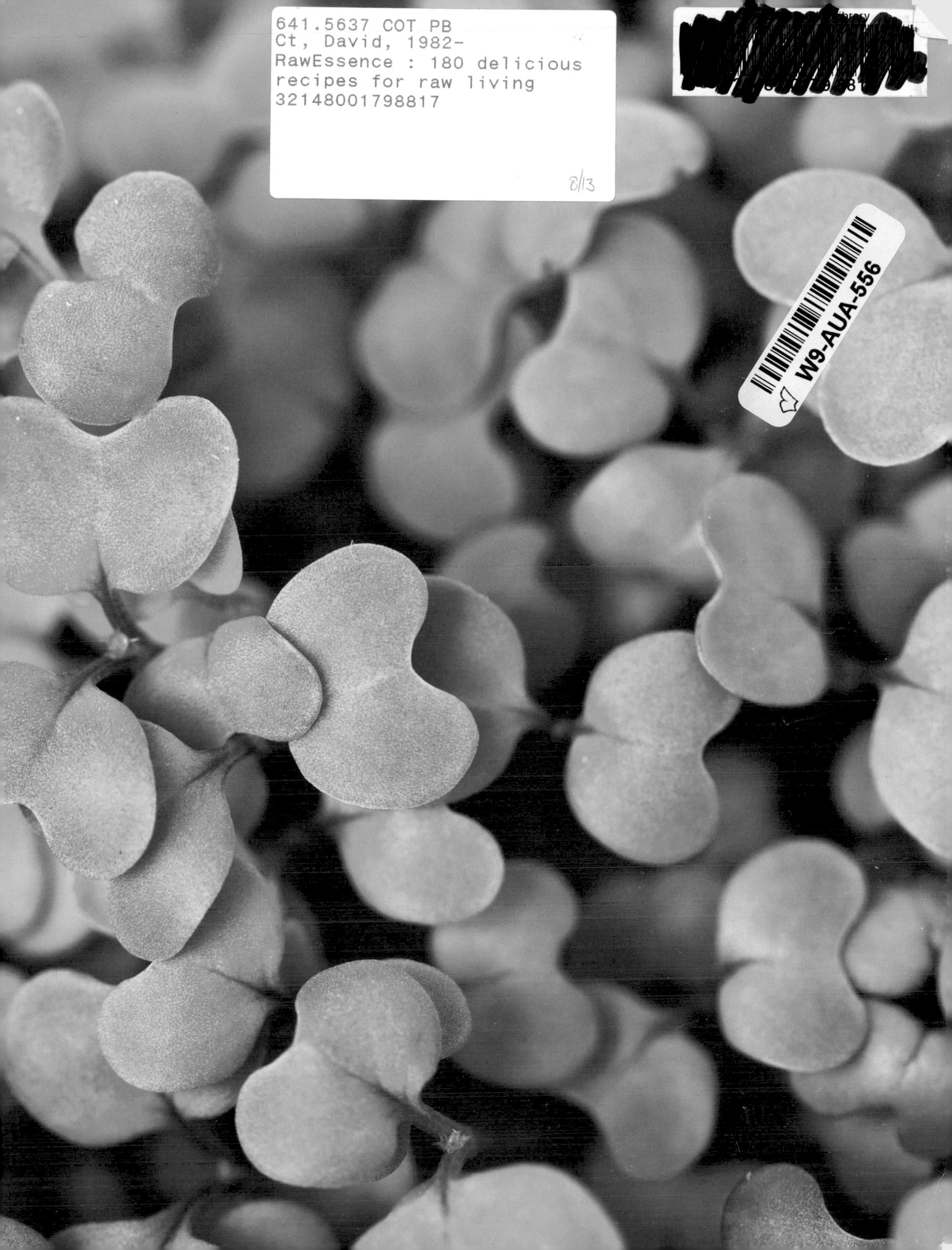

RawEssence
Published originally under the title: *Crudessence*
© 2011, Les Éditions de L'Homme, a division of Groupe Sogides inc., subsidiary of Québecor
Media inc. (Montréal, Québec, Canada)
Cover and text design copyright © 2013 Robert Rose Inc.

For complete cataloguing information, see page 223.

Disclaimer

The recipes in this book have been carefully tested by our kitchen and our tasters. To the best of
our knowledge, they are safe and nutritious for ordinary use and users. For those people with food
or other allergies, or who have special food requirements or health issues, please read the
suggested contents of each recipe carefully and determine whether or not they may create a
problem for you. All recipes are used at the risk of the consumer.

We cannot be responsible for any hazards, loss or damage that may occur as a result of any
recipe use.

For those with special needs, allergies, requirements or health problems, in the event of any
doubt, please contact your medical adviser prior to the use of any recipe.

Design and Production: PageWave Graphics Inc.
Editor: Carol Sherman
Translator: Donna Vekteris
Consulting Editor: Judith Finlayson
Copy Editor: Karen Campbell-Sheviak
Photography: Mathieu Dupuis
Prop and Food Styling: Luce Meunier
Digital Image Processing: Mélanie Sabourin
Kitchen and Table Accessories: Linen Chest, La Maison d'Émilie and Ares

Page layout adapted from Crudessence, *designed by Ann-Sophie Caouette and formatted
by Chantal Landry*

Cover image: Cheese Roll (see page 52)

We acknowledge the financial support of the Government of Canada through the Book Publishing
Industry Development Program (BPIDP) for our publishing activities.

Published by Robert Rose Inc.
120 Eglinton Avenue East, Suite 800, Toronto, Ontario, Canada, M4P 1E2
Tel: (416) 322-6552 Fax: (416) 322-6936
www.robertrose.ca

Printed and bound in Canada

1 2 3 4 5 6 7 8 9 TCP 21 20 19 18 17 16 15 14 13

RawEssence

180 DELICIOUS RECIPES FOR RAW LIVING

DAVID CÔTÉ & MATHIEU GALLANT

Robert
ROSE

Contents

The flavor of our mission

This book is designed for all those who:
- love to discover new flavors;
- dare to step off the beaten path;
- wish to live a long life;
- are ready to make changes in their lives;
- would like to eat better but don't know where to begin;
- are striving for optimum health;
- want to make more environmentally friendly choices;
- wish to achieve higher levels of physical performance;
- want to lose weight or maintain a healthy weight;
- are gluten-intolerant or not;
- are lactose-intolerant or not;
- are vegetarian or not;
- are learning to prepare food, love to prepare food or don't like being in the kitchen at all, except to eat.

Our restaurant Crudessence was born out of a desire to live life to the fullest: a need for two friends to share their passions, common vision and experiences; and a propensity to move forward ever further, to exceed the comfortable bounds of the familiar and find a richer and more profound life experience.

After years of travels and personal studies, we were both hoping to share our experiences and vision of the world. In spite of very different paths, we had the same impression: that it is possible to do more with less, and that human beings have incredible potential waiting to be developed.

We decided to create a project for healthy eating, offering people not only high quality products and services but also the chance to conduct an experiment in live food. This adventure allows the explorer who dares to embark on it to become a living laboratory and to soon begin to sense the power of life. The experiment speaks for itself!

Our travels have given us a certain critical perspective on the world and our youth has allowed us to have a slightly revolutionary attitude. Like many of you, we are aware of environmental destruction, the industrialization of food, deteriorating public health and many other problems today.

At the same time, we see the emergence of a profound desire for change and a genuine search for viable solutions. It is now possible to make a meaningful transition in how we live. We felt the urge to be part of this wave of positive solutions and to give our best!

The Crudessence adventure had its humble beginnings in the summer of 2007, in the form of a small catering service and kombucha (fermented tea) brewery (see page 128). An equal mixture of passion, intuition, invaluable encounters and relentless work soon transformed our concept into a well-established company. Four years later, our team of 70 employees is busy spreading our joie de vivre at two restaurants, two health food counters and a catering service for individuals and companies. Crudessence also has an online food shop and, at each of its establishments, a cooking school, the Academy of Living Foods, with a very elaborate program. Finally, Crudessence has a kombucha brewery that distributes health beverages in Canada. How quickly we have grown! Surely it's a sign that the vitality of our company comes from the vitality of our diet! The fuel that we consume can, indeed, throw a wrench into the gears or it can propel us.

The promises of the living diet:
- a return to optimal health in a natural way;
- rapid regeneration of tissue;
- heightened mental concentration and renewed creativity;
- deep, restorative sleep;
- clear skin and natural beauty;
- sparkling eyes and undeniable presence;
- healthy weight and a well-proportioned figure;
- a greater zest for life and the desire to push one's limits;
- a new perspective on life, positive change;
- a direct impact on the economy and environmental health.

Instead of going to war against what is negative, we have chosen to nourish what is positive and to celebrate life.

And so, Crudessence was born.

In fact, the realm of food is an obvious choice for sending a message in a special way. We are aware that food affects every aspect of life, economic, socially and environmentally. As well, food often influences our state of being. Are our physical and mental health not directly linked to our intrinsic relationship with the living? This is why living food becomes a marvelous tool for changing the world! Here, the well-known and paradoxically simplistic adage applies perfectly:

We are what we eat...

Our future depends on what we will eat...

The living food experiment brings us quickly to the conclusion that the quality of the foods consumed affects the quality of life. Try the experiment. Fill up your car with unrefined gasoline and you will get mediocre performance, pollution and a clogged engine. Fill up with refined, high-octane gasoline and you will have surprising performance, little pollution and a clean engine, right?

Or, build your house with worn-out materials, unqualified workers and bad tools: the house won't cost you a lot, but it will rapidly deteriorate. On the other hand, if you build your house with the best there is to offer, you'll be able to enjoy it with your family much longer!

Today, we present you with this same kind of logic on your plate and in your body. Living food is high in nutrients, enzymes, minerals, proteins and vitamins and also contains life. Everything you need to grow and achieve your full potential!

Does that interest you? We suggest that you simply try it!

— Mathieu and David

crudessence

Raw food in the world

The history of the movement and its principal players: RawEssence vision of food as opposed to the usual dogmatism

From the raw food diet to the live food diet

The idea of having an uncooked vegan diet is not a recent one. Humans are, in fact, the only creatures on Earth who cook their food. The physiological constitution of humans, however, is certainly that of primates. Their digestive systems are designed to function best by consuming fruits, leafy vegetables, algae and seaweed, nuts and seeds. The digestive system of primates is not suited to large-scale consumption of meat or cereals, and certainly not chemicals or products that have been transformed or genetically modified. The indubitably perfect and uncontestable logic of nature is our master and it encourages us to embrace it in our daily choices.

Man had the genius to survive the Ice Age thanks to hunting and developed sedentary civilizations thanks to growing cereal. Cooking was thus very useful for transforming these foods by destroying pathogenic bacteria and aiding absorption. To adapt, man adapted to his environment, but his digestive system did not change.

Once man's survival was ensured, the meat was still there, but it was no longer vital; even Pythagoras, the celebrated mathematician of ancient Greece, founded an intellectual brotherhood in which a vegetarian diet was a prerequisite. Hippocrates, one of his students, now considered the father of medicine, was thought to have followed a vegan diet that was for the most part uncooked, and once said: "Your food should be your remedy." A declaration that is still so important today!

Cereals, which served humanity so well by stabilizing local production and restoring food security, are now subject to reinterpretation. Green plants, sprouts, fruits and vegetables are much denser in nutrients, more easily digested and more curative than grains. Isn't it a sign that allergies and intolerances, especially to gluten, are on the rise? We're not talking about eliminating grains here, but restoring them to their rightful place.

> The RawEssence vision of the live food diet is different from that of the raw food diet.

The raw food diet has become a fascinating topic. It can be seen as fashionable since it is innovative and turns old ideas upside down. It can also be seen as a powerful social movement because it is based on scientific reasoning, answers a need and carries a message of hope.

The trend is, in fact, quite a powerful one: a number of celebrities follow it (Leonardo DiCaprio, Demi Moore and Woody Harrelson, among others) and praise its benefits. Raw food health centers are emerging all over the world, presenting this cuisine with curative powers that offers a surprising healing rate (often far beyond traditional medicine). In large cities in the world, small green oases are also appearing. Little by little, an international community is growing, while literature and websites are multiplying. The great wave of the green diet!

In California, the cradle of many revolutionary movements, the live food diet is no exception. Since 1990, juice bars and raw food restaurants have been appearing on the landscape, inviting Americans and the world to discover the keys to this science of natural health, of which here are the main principles.

The notion of pH: The body's chemical balance is crucial. Degenerative illnesses develop naturally in an acidic and stagnant terrain. Life is liberated in an alkaline terrain. On his deathbed, Louis Pasteur expired with these last words: "The pathogen is nothing; the terrain is everything." This simple phrase illustrates that by balancing one's pH through lifestyle and diet, it is possible to prevent inflammation and degeneration.

The importance of enzymes: Cooking destroys these life-building agents, which play a large role in digestion and in repairing the body. Raw foods, in their perfect form, abound in enzymes. Certain practices in the raw food diet, such as fermentation and germination, actually attempt to multiply and preserve this enzymatic power. The best friends of digestion are enzymes!

The abundance of nutrients: Cooking destroys most of the delicate nutrients in foods. Vitamins, phytonutrients, enzymes, hormones, water and whole sugars are found combined in the macromolecules that cooking damages.

A complete source of amino acids: The paradigm of the need for animal protein is a thing of the past. In dietetics today, it is now understood that proteins are complex chains of amino acids and that a green, diversified vegan diet abounds in them. The plant proteins in leafy vegetables, shoots and sprouted legumes are easy to digest and thus provide better energy output. Consuming a wide variety of plants ensures a supply of all the amino acids essential to the construction of complete proteins.

Detoxification: According to research, the body of the average American accumulates heavy metals, chemical products and other acidulent inorganic molecules. Most phytonutrients and minerals in raw foods help the eliminatory organs (colon, kidneys, skin and lungs) to obtain all they need to do their work, expel these toxins and regain health.

Better blood circulation: Thanks to the large quantity of water and chlorophyll consumed in a raw meal and a lower calorie content than the classic North American meal, digestion requires less blood, thus leaving more for the regeneration and oxygenation of the muscles and brain.

An increase in nutrients: Certain techniques such as soaking, germination and fermentation increase the nutritive value and bioavailability of nutrients. Vitamins increase; fats and proteins are simplified.

Chlorophyll is the basis of life: This pigment is vital on the planet. It transforms solar energy into simple sugar by joining the carbon and hydrogen atoms in water and expelling oxygen. For our part, we consume these sugars, then oxygen, to create energy in our cells and thus expel carbon, which will be turned back into sugar…the magic of life!

A surplus of energy: Once the adventurer is well nourished, digestion facilitated, pH balanced and the body detoxified and regenerated, the adventurer finds himself or herself with a lot of surplus energy. This energy is now available for achieving one's wildest dreams and living life to the fullest! The most complicated thing is not to change one's diet, but to manage all this energy well!

Eating life according to RawEssence

Through direct experience, we fully embrace the principles of the raw food diet and apply its precepts in our kitchens. Through our personal experience, however, and that of thousands of our students and customers, we take pleasure in extrapolating these ideas and adding our piece to the jigsaw puzzle.

> To us, the raw food diet is a diet…
> While live food is an art of living.

An environmentally responsible diet: If the raw foods on our plate contribute to the deterioration of the planet, can we call them "living"? The live food diet is concerned with the ecological, economical and human footprint of foods. To us, an organic, vegan and local diet leads to well-being without the aftertaste of exploitation.

A revolutionary political act: The power that foods have to change the world by directing buying power toward responsible enterprises is immense. Feeding the local economy and weaving new economic ties are essential to breaking out of the globalization dead end. To eat is to vote with each mouthful — a gentle revolution with each plate and for the pleasure of it!

Becoming one's own nutritionist through experience: RawEssence invites individuals to "measure themselves" according to food science by performing live experiments — eating and listening to the body, feeling the effects of foods and creating a personal diet according to how one feels, not according to what specialists, the media or hearsay have dictated. Experimentation is the key to food freedom. There is nothing more satisfying than waking up one morning and sensing what your body wishes to consume.

Participate in global well-being: Our enterprise is, for us, a way of participating in humanity's transition to healthier living habits. We have a great need to reposition ourselves as a community for a more viable and responsible future. With our restaurants, shops, food preparation courses and active community, we are committed to what we consider a more harmonious future for all. Food is, in this way, a perfect excuse to become involved!

Artistic research: To us, culinary art is a great art — a sensual vehicle for nourishing ourselves with beauty and pleasure. That is why we take pleasure in making healthy food so delicious and inspiring people to rediscover the pleasure of eating with love and sharing meals together. Eating healthy is not just curative, it's also recreational — a recreational game of life!

In short, our culinary approach is not a diet, a regime or food dogma. It is a philosophy and a lifestyle whose goal is to give individuals the power to rediscover their health and joie de vivre by changing their perspective on this seemingly banal act of eating.

We do not encourage you to change your habits overnight but rather to commit to trying the experiment. Slowly, the body will recognize it and ask for more!

Slowly adding what is good is our only doctrine. The non-essential will vanish by itself. Just one thing: get ready to take a bite out of life!

The fundamentals of RawEssence

Our Basic Food Values

Organic

The human body, just like the environment, is a perfect ecosystem in constant search of equilibrium. Of course, we alone are responsible for our body's equilibrium, but collectively we are responsible for that of our environment. To us, choosing and encouraging organic farming means respecting and maintaining this harmony that is so precious to life.

Obviously, we do not want petroleum-based ingredients in our food or our children's food, or petroleum products in the air that we breathe and the water that we drink. Choosing organic is a direct act, in this sense.

Conventional foods, which are full of fertilizer and chemical pesticides and often irradiated or genetically modified, are, according to the agro-food industry, comparable to organic foods in terms of nutritional value. Nevertheless, we all know that whatever destroys the soil and the environment will eventually end up in a food that will directly or indirectly harm human beings.

For us, live food is food that has encouraged life on its journey, from the seed to our dish, passing through the hands of the workers and ending up in every cell of our body; 100 per cent organic is an ideal, of course, but each step in this direction is held in high regard!

Local

Eating local is a very "live" act. By directly encouraging the food producers and transformers in our region, we play an active role, weaving a social fabric that benefits everyone. Local economic ties are, in fact, the fibers of an important network, providing work for our community while investing in the sustainable development of our region and our country.

Locally grown foods allow us to avoid overseas transportation and help prevent the development of international monoculture and food speculation. Each country and region should be sovereign over its food without being deprived of a little enjoyment from international exotic foods. In this way, foreign products become delicious exceptions, but not daily basics.

What's more, it is such a pleasure to personally know one's gardener, who is so proud to offer his or her creations, or to have one's own vegetable garden, a tray of young shoots, sprouting jars and lacto-fermentation — it's the micro-local way. Crudessence is happy to be part of a rooftop-garden project in Montreal. The 150 planters we have today are sure to yield a horn of plenty — in vegetables and in experience!

Nothing against globalization, but all for localization.

Vegan

Today, thanks to the Internet and many whistle-blowing films, the atrocious living conditions of livestock destined for food are no longer a secret. Meat gets plenty of bad press. Still, it is up to each of us to assess the impact of our consumption in order to change our entrenched habits.

Here is a short list of impacts:
- **Deforestation for grazing;**
- **Cruelty of slaughterhouses;**
- **Use of growth hormones;**
- **Depletion of oceans;**
- **Use of resources (water and grain) to feed livestock;**
- **High concentration of pesticides;**
- **Impact on human health.**

For our part, we offer you delicious solutions. The plant world abounds in nutrients for our diet. Our kitchen is therefore completely bare of products from animal sources and their derivatives. And our recipes, without eggs, milk, butter, cheese, and seafood, for example, are so good that one quickly forgets they are vegan.

A little reminder for those who go suddenly from a carnivorous diet to a plant-based diet: favor fresh green vegetables and fruits, and avoid an excess of pasta, breads, potatoes and fried foods. Eat live food and you will gain so much by it!

Gluten and allergen-free

Have you noticed recently that allergies and food intolerances have increased in a draconian way? More and more, the finger is being pointed at gluten, peanuts, dairy products, soy, pesticides, chemical additives, colorants and refined sugar. These ingredients, transformed so much by the food industry and over-consumed by the population, are perhaps sending us a message: that it's time to go back to what's natural!

Economically committed

The central gear of the economy is food. Food runs the world! And because everyone "votes" on a daily basis with his or her purchases, we have committed ourselves to this economic sector as food revolutionaries. Because trends in the industry are guided by choices made by the population, we all have the responsibility of supporting, through our purchasing power, companies that encourage what is good for everyone. Paying more for local organic food is a loaded concept today. It is an act that speaks, an inspirational drop of water that contributes significantly to a torrent of change.

It is this purchasing power that will feed the producer, the wholesaler and the grocer and oblige them to respect our values. It is possible to nourish life simply, recognizing the power of our choices.

Medicine in my dish!

That's right! In bygone days, food and medicine were one and the same. Today, our produce has been modified to be saturated with water, to be more colorful and sweeter, to stay fresh longer, to resist herbicides and to be aesthetically perfect. Unfortunately, it has not been modified to be more nutritious or medicinal.

In this area, we cannot compete with what nature has prepared for us. Super foods, medicinal herbs, wild plants and even so-called "weeds" are veritable treasure troves of nutrition. Not only do they grow without man's intervention, but they are also extremely high in nutrients and in beneficial chemical compounds. Often, they manage to be nutritious, preventative and curative. They are, after all, the basis of pharmacopoeia.

It is not surprising that populations from every part of the world have an exhaustive natural pharmacopoeia and that this precious knowledge is passed down from one generation to the next. Today, we are responsible for preserving this heritage and popularizing it.

And so, in this book you will find many "new" ancient ingredients. The wisdom and the medicines they contain, which are often hidden behind their bewitching flavors, will be honored — it's about staying healthy without giving up the pleasures of the table!

Seeds, grains and nuts

ALMONDS
high in calcium
and alkalinizing

WALNUTS
high in minerals
and vitamin B6

PUMPKIN SEEDS
complete protein and
antiparasitic

**SUNFLOWER
SEEDS**
economical and
abundant in
vitamin E

CASHEW NUTS
silky and versatile

FLAX
high in omega-3
and facilitates
intestinal transit

PECANS
high in zinc; positive
effect on cholesterol

**SESAME
SEEDS**
very high in calcium

PISTACHIOS
high in potassium
and copper

HEMP
local seed containing
all the amino acids

BRAZIL NUTS
preserve the Amazon
rainforest and contain
selenium

**MACADAMIA
NUTS**
contain
excellent
fatty acids

QUINOA
alkalinizing seed
high in protein

CHIA
nutritious gelling
agent and omega-3
champion

BUCKWHEAT
complete protein that
is easy to germinate

Sweeteners

COCONUT BUTTER
puréed coconut flakes;
perfect for desserts

YOUNG COCONUTS
source of natural
electrolytes

**POWDERED
COCONUT MILK**
silky texture

CRANBERRIES
clean urinary
tract and are an
antioxidant

GRATED COCONUT
fiber and good
saturated fat;
versatile in cuisine

BLUEBERRIES
local antioxidant

COCONUT OIL
nutritious, antibacterial,
easily metabolized

MAPLE SYRUP
abundant in
minerals

AGAVE NECTAR
cactus sap composed
of fructose and inulin

FIGS
abundant in vitamin B3 and
potassium

APRICOTS
high in
beta-carotene

LIQUID STEVIA
concentrated stevia
extract

STEVIA
glucose-free
sweetener

DATES
versatile and economical
sweetener

Super foods

CACAO NIBS
raw cacao seeds that are high
in magnesium

GOJI BERRIES
very high in vitamin C and
other antioxidants

COCOA BUTTER
abundant in vitamin E
and excellent for the skin

COCOA POWDER
antioxidant and stimulant

PHYSALIS
source of
flavonoids, pectin
and vitamin A

MULBERRIES
contain resveratrol
and iron

MATCHA
powerful
energizing
antioxidant

SPIRULINA
microalga high in protein
and chlorophyll

BEE POLLEN
40% protein; whole food

CHLORELLA
microalga containing
vitamin B12 and minerals

MESQUITE
regulates
glycemia

MACA
hormonal
adaptogen and
aphrodisiac

LUCUMA
probiotic
polysaccharide
and thickener

Other

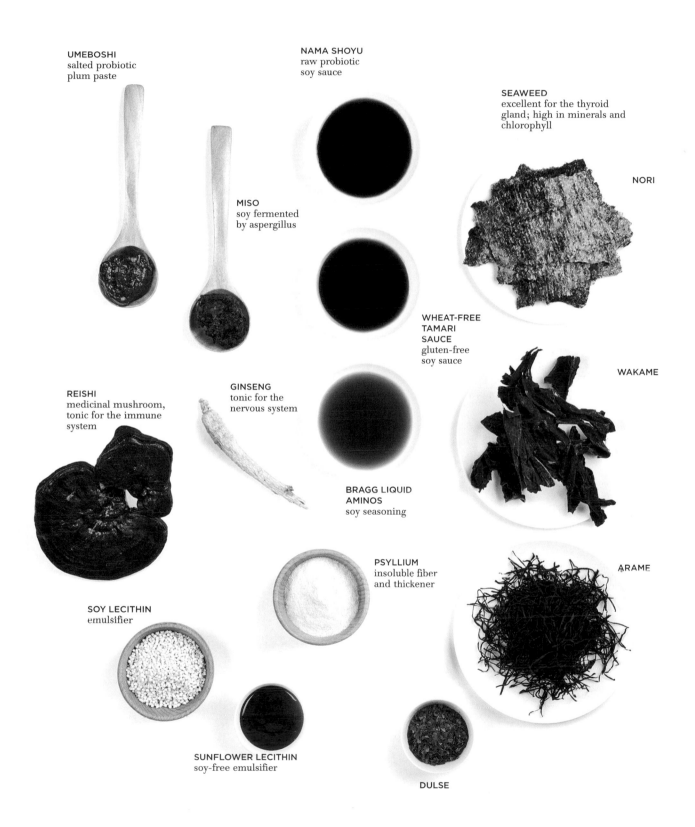

UMEBOSHI
salted probiotic
plum paste

NAMA SHOYU
raw probiotic
soy sauce

SEAWEED
excellent for the thyroid
gland; high in minerals and
chlorophyll

NORI

MISO
soy fermented
by aspergillus

**WHEAT-FREE
TAMARI
SAUCE**
gluten-free
soy sauce

WAKAME

REISHI
medicinal mushroom,
tonic for the immune
system

GINSENG
tonic for the
nervous system

**BRAGG LIQUID
AMINOS**
soy seasoning

PSYLLIUM
insoluble fiber
and thickener

ARAME

SOY LECITHIN
emulsifier

SUNFLOWER LECITHIN
soy-free emulsifier

DULSE

Techniques

Soaking and germination

Most of the seeds and nuts used in our recipes have been presoaked to start the germination process. Water, the main key of life, gives the seed the illusion of rainfall, and that it is time to start growing into a plant. It is thus possible to garden in the wintertime, on the kitchen counter, and to draw many benefits from it.

The purpose of all seeds and nuts

Soaking is the first part of germination, when enzymes are activated and the breaking-down process begins. It takes 20 minutes to 12 hours, depending on the type of seed. Germination requires between 24 hours and several days and transforms the seed into a food that is easy to digest and extremely high in minerals and nutrients.

Jar germination

Utensils
- Glass jar (jam jar)
- Filter (piece of fine screen or cheesecloth)
- Elastic band

1. Place seeds in the bottom of jar. For small seeds (alfalfa, clover, radish, etc.), use 1 tbsp (15 mL) for a 1-cup (250 mL) jar. For large seeds (lentils, azuki, buckwheat, etc.), use ⅓ cup (75 mL) for a 1-cup (250 mL) jar.

2. Fasten the filter you are using to mouth of jar with elastic band, then rinse seeds in warm water to remove all dust.

3. Fill jar with filtered water and let soak 8 hours (overnight) or required amount of time for the seed (see soaking and germination table on page 20).

4. After soaking period, pour out water, rinse, then place jar upside down on a dish rack.

5. Rinse 2 to 3 times per day, drain and place on dish rack. The sprouts need to breathe. Let germinate for the required amount of time, according to the types of seeds.

6. Rinse thoroughly and drain before eating.

TIP
Keeps 4 to 7 days in the refrigerator.

Note
- Pure water is essential for the soaking period. For rinsing, tap water is sufficient.
- Darkness stimulates the growth of the sprouts in the first few days. Put the jar in a cupboard (as long as it is well aerated) or simply cover it with a dishcloth.
- After the third day, alfalfa and clover can be rinsed just once a day. This will help them keep longer and make them crunchier.

Benefits of germination:
- Elimination of enzyme inhibitors naturally found in seeds;
- Breaking down of proteins into amino acids and fats into fatty acids;
- Hydration of food for easy digestion;
- Increased vitamin content;
- Increased bioavailability of nutrients;
- Reduction of the pancreas's need to produce enzymes;
- Considerable budgetary savings;
- Creation of chlorophyll.

Soaking and Germination Table

Variety	Soaking period (hours)	Shoot length at harvest time (inches/cm)	Germination period (days)
Alfalfa	6	1–1½ in (2.5–4 cm)	4–5
Almonds and nuts	12	–	Do not sprout.
Amaranth	2	¼ in (0.5 cm)	1–3
Azuki	12	½–1 in (1–2.5 cm)	2–3
Barley	12	¼–¾ in (0.5–2 cm)	3–4
Buckwheat (with hulls)	0.5	3½ in (8.5 cm)	5–6
Chickpeas	24	¼–1 in (0.5–2.5 cm)	2–3
Clover	6	1–1½ in (2.5–4 cm)	4–5
Coral lentils	6	½ in (1 cm)	2–4
Fenugreek	8	¾ to 1 in (2–2.5 cm)	1–3
Kamut	8	¼–¾ in (0.5–2 cm)	1–3
Lentils	8	½–1 in (1–2.5 cm)	1–3
Mung beans	8	¾–1 in (2–2.5 cm)	2–6
Oats	12	¼–¾ in (0.5–2 cm)	2–3
Pumpkin seeds	4	–	–
Quinoa	8	¼–1¼ in (0.5–3 cm)	0–1
Rye	8	¼–¾ in (0.5–2 cm)	2–3
Sesame seeds (shelled)	4	1	–
Spelt	10	¼–¾ in (0.5–2 cm)	1–3
Sunflower seeds (shelled)	4	1	–
Triticale	16	¼–¾ in (0.5–2 cm)	2–3
Whole millet	10	¼ in (0.5 cm)	3–5
Wild rice	36	–	Does not sprout.

Table for young shoots in earth

Variety	Soaking period (hours)	Shoot length at harvest time (inches/cm)	Germination period (days)
Broccoli	4–6	1½–2 in (4–5 cm)	2.5
Cabbage	4–6	1½–2 in (4–5 cm)	2.5
Carrot	4–6	3¼–3½ in (8–8.5 cm)	4
Corn	8–10	2–2½ in (5–6 cm)	10
Green peas	8–10	1½–2 in (4–5 cm)	10
Leek	12	4–6 in (10–15 cm)	3–4
Mustard	0.5–2	1¼–1½ in (3–4 cm)	3.5
Radish	6–8	1¼–1½ in (3–4 cm)	3.5
Sunflower seeds	8–10	3¼ in (8 cm)	5–6
(in shell)	8–10	2–2½ in (5–6 cm)	8
Watercress	8	1½–2 in (4–5 cm)	1.5
Wheat (hard or soft)	8	2–2½ in (5–6 cm)	20

Shoots in soil

Utensils

- ¾- to 1¼-inch (2 to 3 cm) deep container (soup dish, tray, etc.)
- organic quality soil (ideally with earthworm fertilizer)
- spray bottle
- organic seeds with husks: sunflower, buckwheat, hard wheat, barley, watercress, broccoli, onions, cabbage, etc.

1. Start by soaking seeds in jars for 8 hours or required length of time (see Soaking and Germination Table, left). After soaking, pour off water and rinse seeds. They are now ready to be planted.

2. Fill a container with soil and pack it down slightly. Spray surface of soil to moisten it.

3. Spread wet seeds over soil with a fork. They should lie close together but not overlap.

4. Cover with a heavy lid, tray or plate. Store in a dark place for 1 to 2 days to give the roots time to grow and for the heads to press on the lid. It is not necessary to water during this period.

5. Remove cover, place the shoots in full light (florescent or sun) and spray soil 2 to 3 times a day, until the shoots reach the optimal length (see table, left).

6. Remove integuments (the seeds' hard coating), cut with scissors and eat.

TIP

Shoots keep 5 to 7 days in the refrigerator.

Nut milks

Tree milk instead of cow milk? Yes! Nuts and seeds can be turned into delicious health drinks! Raw plant milks, which are full of enzymes, vitamins and amino acids, are much easier to digest and lighter than whole nuts and seeds.

With a blender and a filter, nuts or seeds can become nut milk in no time at all. These versatile milks keep 4 days in the refrigerator and can be flavored in a variety of ways. You will find them in recipes for smoothies or to accompany granolas, desserts and hot beverages; they can even be turned into vanilla milk, strawberry milk or chocolate milk! Unlike commercial pasteurized cow's milk, soy milk or nut milk, the milks you prepare at home will be full of life and very nutritious. Our favorite milks? Hemp milk and hazelnut chocolate milk… pure delights! Procedure, in short:

1. Soak 1 cup (250 mL) of your favorite nuts or seeds: almonds, hazelnuts, sesame, pumpkin, Brazil nuts, pecans, hemp, etc., for about 8 hours (or overnight).

2. Drain, then rinse. Discard soaking water.

3. In a blender, grind nuts thoroughly with 4 cups (1 L) of water for 45 seconds.

4. Filter with a nut milk filter or a fine sieve.

That's it, you have milk!

TIPS

If you like it creamier, increase the quantity of nuts per 4 cups (1 L) of water.

The pulp from the seeds or nuts that collects in the filter can be refrigerated or dehydrated and used as flour in other recipes such as cookies and cakes.

Fermentation

Fermentation is a process of increasing nutrients through live microscopic activity. For us, bacteria, enzymes and yeasts turn simple sugars into organic acids and proteins into amino acids while increasing vitamins and digestibility tenfold. Fermentation is also an effective method of conservation and a culinary art that offers a vast palette of textures and surprising flavors. Fermentations all have the following in common: they reinforce the immune system, support intestinal flora and are an invaluable aid to digestion.

The nutritional advantages of fermentation are well known in many civilizations — sauerkraut, lacto-fermentation, kefir, kombucha, yogurt and nut cheese, miso, tamari, tempeh, etc., as well as yeast breads, cured meats, beer, coffee and wine! Fermentations are omnipresent, beneficial and very accessible. Anyone can cultivate this army of "micro chefs" that transform foods for their health benefits. A vast world to rediscover!

Dehydration

Another ancestral culinary process, dehydration is an effective way to preserve all the nutrients in foods. By slowly extracting the water through low-temperature ventilation (105°F/41°C), we avoid cooking and, consequently, the destruction of enzymes and delicate nutrients.

With the help of a dehydrator, we create not only food reserves that are easy to preserve but also a panoply of textures and fortifying flavors. Indeed, dehydration makes it possible to prepare breads, crackers, granolas, chips, crêpes, cookies and a variety of healthy snacks sure to win over those who are reluctant to try the live food diet. The dehydrator is an economical and easy-to-use device that allows plenty of creativity and endless culinary exploration.

The dehydrator will help you to:
- Preserve foods;
- Preserve foods' nutritional value;
- Save money by drying foods you have bought in season;
- Consume dried fruits that have no added sulfites or sugar;
- Achieve the textures you desire through varied drying times;
- Imitate cooked textures and delight your family;
- Replace heavy cereal grains and flours with sprouted seeds;
- Rekindle your culinary passion.

Equipment

Blender

This is the prime, essential piece of equipment in our live food kitchen. A conventional blender of medium quality will do the job quite well. However, if this type of diet suits you well, you will never regret the investment of a few hundred dollars in a good blender; in this case, we recommend the same one we use in our kitchens, the Vitamix. This machine can grind and give your sauces, creams, soups, smoothies, mousses, etc. a silky texture in no time at all. What's more, you can easily make nut flours and nut butters. Using such a powerful motor can transform foods to the point that some nutrients are destroyed in the process. Although this should be taken into consideration, the quantity of green plants, fruits and vegetables that a blender will allow you to consume greatly exceeds the amount of nutrients that may be lost in the process.

Food processor

As the food processor allows you to make spreads and desserts and to prepare vegetables for salads, it will greatly facilitate the preparation of live food on a daily basis. Most brands will do the job very well; choose a simple and sturdy model that will last a long time. In our cooking courses we use a food processor bought at the lowest price possible to demonstrate that it is possible to perform miracles on a small budget! The food processor, like the blender, facilitates digestion because it makes food easier to chew. In fact, raw vegetables, nuts and seeds need to be chewed well to be completely digested. Given our tendency to swallow our foods whole, preparing and refining food is an essential step that compensates for lack of chewing!

Dehydrator

Although there are many dehydrators on the market, we recommend the Excalibur for its efficiency and excellent output. The dehydration times given in this book are for an Excalibur. The Excalibur is a rectangular-shaped dehydrator. There are also ring-shaped ones available but be aware that the time of dehydration might change and the quantities will have to be spread differently. You are not obliged to have a dehydrator to make our recipes. It is possible to dehydrate foods with a conventional oven, leaving the door half open and adjusting the thermostat to the lowest possible temperature. Of course, you won't achieve exactly the same result, but you will be able to perform some interesting tests. A number of convection ovens now offer a dehydrating option. This allows you to experiment with dehydrating, and then consider the purchase of a real dehydrator.

Nonstick dehydrator sheets (aka Teflex sheets): These are permeable, nonstick sheets on which one can pour a liquid mixture. It is possible to use waxed paper to obtain a similar result, except for certain recipes that are too sticky or that make it too difficult to separate the wax paper from the mixture.

Centrifuge and juice extractor

Centrifuges consist of small metal blades that shred vegetables and extract the juice by centrifugation. They work well with all root vegetables, apples, celery, cucumbers and juicy fruits. They cannot, however, extract the precious juice from leafy greens. The slow juice extractor (with endless screw) functions like a juice press. It allows the chlorophyll from leafy vegetables to be extracted without producing heat. The slow extractor is suitable for every other type of vegetable and fruit and makes it possible for us to very easily consume large quantities of vegetables, without the fiber. We do, however, recommend consuming fruits and sweet vegetables with their fiber because fiber slows down digestion and helps prevent a blood sugar imbalance. As for vegetables that are not sweet, there are no limits. Your body will thank you for the abundance of vitamins and minerals in these green alkalinizing juices.

Spiral cut machine

This practical, inexpensive device allows you to cut vegetables into amazing shapes. In an instant, you can cut zucchini or any hard vegetable into spaghetti, half moons or spirals, for example. With just a little "elbow grease," you can make your vegetables attractive to the most reluctant eaters and transform your dishes into gastronomic meals. Zucchini and apples can be eaten as is, but it is better to drain harder vegetables — turnip, beet, sweet potato, squash, daikon (white radish), black radish, etc. — before eating them. To do this, simply cut these vegetables the way you like, add salt, then let them sweat for about 15 minutes; the vegetables will release some of their water and become more tender. Rinse them thoroughly under running water to remove the salt, then eat!

Green juices — the true secret of youth in the live food diet

To learn more about culinary equipment, visit our website: www.crudessence.com

Basic recipes

Ginger Juice

| 3 cups | unpeeled, coarsely chopped gingerroot | 750 mL |
| 3/4 cup | water | 175 mL |

Preparation: 10 minutes
Equipment: juice extractor

Makes 1 1/2 cups (375 mL)

1. Run ginger through juice extractor twice to extract all juice.

2. Dilute juice with water.

TIPS

To freeze, simply pour mixture into ice cube trays. Use the ice cubes in recipes.

To increase this recipe, always add an equal proportion of water to the ginger juice obtained from extraction.

Keeps 3 weeks in the refrigerator or 6 months in an ice cube tray in the freezer.

Sprouted Buckwheat

| 2 lbs | buckwheat groats | 1 kg |

Soaking: 30 minutes
Preparation: 10 minutes
Germination: 24 to 36 hours
Dehydration: about 12 hours
Equipment: dehydrator

Makes 6 1/2 cups (1.625 L) buckwheat groats
Makes 6 cups (1.5 L) dehydrated buckwheat

1. *Soaking:* In a large container, cover buckwheat with water and let soak for 30 minutes.

2. *Sprouting:* After soaking, pour buckwheat into a sieve and rinse thoroughly. Place sieve into a large container to collect excess water. Cover with a clean dishcloth: germination will take place in the sieve. Let germinate for 24 to 36 hours, rinsing 2 to 3 times per day. The buckwheat will form mucilage and turn sticky. This is natural and it is not necessary to rinse it any more to remove this gluey appearance.

3. The buckwheat is ready when it has grown to the height of the seed. The buckwheat can now be used as is, but if you want to preserve it, it is preferable to dehydrate it.

4. *Dehydration (optional):* Spread the buckwheat on the racks of the dehydrator and dry at 105°F (41°C) for 8 to 12 hours. The buckwheat is sufficiently dry when the stem turns to powder under the pressure of the fingers.

TIPS

Keeps moist for 3 to 5 days in the refrigerator.

Keeps dry for 4 months at room temperature in an airtight container.

Date Paste

2½ cups	fresh or dried seedless dates (see Tips, below)	625 mL
1½ cups	water	375 mL

Soaking: 4 to 5 hours
Preparation: 20 minutes
Equipment: food processor

Makes 6½ cups (1.625 L)

1. *Soaking:* In a container, cover dates with water and let soak for 2 hours. Press down thoroughly so all dates are moistened. Cover with a weight, if necessary.

2. Once dates are thoroughly softened, place them along with their soaking water in the food processor and mix until a paste is obtained that is as uniform, sticky and smooth as possible.

TIPS

Dates are used as a fruit paste base because they are sweet, have a relatively neutral flavor and are cheap. It is, however, possible to make fruit paste in the same fashion and same proportions using other dried fruits (grapes, cranberries, apricots, figs, etc.)

Keeps 3 months in the refrigerator.

Garlic Purée

2 cups	whole cloves fresh garlic, core removed	500 mL
½ cup	sunflower oil	125 mL

Preparation: peeling + 10 minutes
Equipment: food processor

Makes 1½ cups (375 mL)

1. In food processor, combine garlic cloves and oil and blend into a smooth purée.

TIPS

To peel garlic more easily: break the heads and soak the cloves for about 1 hour in warm water.

Keeps 3 weeks in the refrigerator or 6 months in the freezer.

Beverages

Pure Almond Milk

1 to 1½ cups	unpeeled almonds	250 to 375 mL
4 cups	water	1 L

Soaking: 8 hours
Preparation: 5 minutes
Equipment: blender, milk filter

Makes 4 1-cup (250 mL) portions

1. *Soaking:* In a bowl, soak almonds in water to cover for 8 hours. Rinse thoroughly and discard soaking water.

2. In blender, combine almonds and water and blend for a few minutes to obtain a white, creamy liquid. If necessary, start by grinding almonds in half the amount of water called for.

3. Filter milk through a nylon or cotton milk filter. Reserve pulp for future recipes; it will keep in the refrigerator for 5 to 7 days.

TIP

Keeps 3 to 4 days in the refrigerator in an airtight container.

Vanilla Hemp Milk

1 cup	shelled hemp seeds	250 mL
4 cups	water	1 L
1 tsp	alcohol-free vanilla essence	5 mL
2 tbsp	agave nectar or maple syrup	30 mL
⅛ tsp	salt	0.5 mL

Preparation: 5 minutes
Equipment: blender

Makes 4 1-cup (250 mL) portions

1. In a blender, combine all ingredients and blend to a creamy milk. The hemp seeds will dissolve almost completely, so it is not necessary to filter the milk (see page 21).

TIP

Keeps 3 to 4 days in the refrigerator in an airtight container.

Brazil Nut Goji Milk

2 cups	Brazil nuts	500 mL
1/3 cup	goji berries	75 mL
4 cups	water	1 L
2 tbsp	agave nectar	30 mL
Pinch	sea salt	Pinch
1/2 tsp	ground cinnamon	2 mL
1/8 tsp	cayenne pepper (optional)	0.5 mL

Soaking: 12 hours (optional)
Preparation: 5 minutes
Equipment: blender; milk filter

Makes 4 portions

1. *Soaking (optional):* In a bowl, soak Brazil nuts in water to cover for 12 hours, then rinse thoroughly. Discard soaking water. Soak goji berries for 1 hour, then drain. Save their soaking water as liquid for another smoothie.

2. In blender, combine all ingredients and blend for a few minutes to obtain a colorful, creamy liquid. If necessary, start by blending Brazil nuts and goji berries in half the water called for.

3. Filter milk through a nylon or cotton milk filter. Save pulp for future recipes; it will keep in the refrigerator for 5 to 7 days.

TIP

Keeps 3 to 4 days in the refrigerator in an airtight container.

Macao Smoothie

1/3 cup	Brazil nuts	75 mL
1 2/3 cups	water	400 mL
3	bananas	3
1/4 cup	cocoa powder	60 mL
2 tsp	maca powder	10 mL
4 tbsp	Date Paste (page 25) or 4 seedless dates	60 mL
1 tbsp	melted coconut oil	15 mL
1/8 tsp	sea salt	0.5 mL

Soaking: 12 hours (optional)
Preparation: 10 minutes
Equipment: blender, milk filter

Makes 2 portions

1. *Soaking (optional):* In a bowl, soak Brazil nuts in water to cover for 12 hours, then rinse thoroughly. Discard soaking water.

2. Make a milk with Brazil nuts and water (see recipe, left).

3. In blender, combine milk and remaining ingredients and blend into a thick smoothie.

TIPS

To drink chilled, use frozen fruits or replace some of the water with ice cubes.

Keeps 2 days in the refrigerator in an airtight container.

Pretty Green Smoothie

3	leaves kale	3
1/2 cup	packed fresh parsley (leaves and stems)	125 mL
1 1/2 cups	water	375 mL
1 1/2	bananas	1 1/2
1 cup	chopped pineapple pieces	250 mL
3 tbsp	Date Paste (page 25) or 3 seedless dates	45 mL
1/4 cup	shelled hemp seeds	60 mL
1/8 tsp	sea salt	0.5 mL

Preparation: 10 minutes
Equipment: blender

Makes 2 portions

1. In blender, combine kale, parsley and water and blend into a green paste.
2. Add remaining ingredients and blend until smooth.

TIPS

To drink chilled, use frozen fruits or replace some of the water with ice cubes.

Keeps 2 days in the refrigerator in an airtight container

Loco Local Smoothie

1 1/4 cups	water	300 mL
2	apples, cored and cubed	2
1/2 cup	blueberries	125 mL
1/2 cup	fresh or dried cranberries	125 mL
6	strawberries, trimmed	6
1 tbsp	maple syrup	15 mL

Preparation: 10 minutes
Equipment: blender

Makes 2 portions

1. In blender, combine all ingredients and blend until smooth.

TIPS

To drink chilled, use frozen fruits or replace some of the water with ice cubes.

Keeps 2 days in the refrigerator in an airtight container.

Soft Green Smoothie

1/3 cup	unpeeled almonds	75 mL
1 1/2 cups	water	375 mL
2	bananas	2
2 cups	spinach	500 mL
10	mint leaves	10
2 tbsp	Date Paste (page 25) or 2 seedless dates	30 mL
1/2 tsp	alcohol-free vanilla essence	2 mL
1/8 tsp	ground cayenne pepper	0.5 mL
1/8 tsp	sea salt	0.5 mL

Soaking: 8 hours
Preparation: 15 minutes
Equipment: blender, milk filter

Makes 2 portions

1. *Soaking:* In a bowl, soak unpeeled almonds in water to cover for 8 hours. Rinse thoroughly and discard soaking water.

2. Make a milk with almonds and water (see Pure Almond Milk, page 28).

3. In blender, combine half the milk and remaining ingredients and blend into a thick, uniform paste.

4. Add remaining milk and blend into a smoothie.

TIPS

To drink chilled, use frozen fruits or replace some of the water with ice cubes.

Keeps 2 days in the refrigerator in an airtight container.

Power Smoothie

1/4 cup	coconut butter	60 mL
2 tbsp	hemp protein	30 mL
2 tsp	maca powder	10 mL
1 1/2 tbsp	goji berries	22 mL
1 1/2 tbsp	mulberries	22 mL
1 1/2 tbsp	dried chia seeds	22 mL
1 tbsp	mesquite powder	15 mL
2	peeled oranges	2
1 1/2	bananas	1 1/2
2 cups	water, divided	500 mL

Optional

1 tbsp	bee pollen	15 mL
1 tsp	matcha powder	5 mL

Preparation: 5 minutes
Equipment: blender

Makes 2 portions

1. In blender, combine all ingredients and half the water and blend into a thick, uniform paste.

2. Add remaining water and blend into a smoothie. Add bee pollen and matcha powder, if desired.

TIPS

To drink chilled, use frozen fruits or replace some of the water with ice cubes.

Keeps 2 days in the refrigerator in an airtight container.

Hard Green Juice

2	apples	2
½	bulb fennel (with leaves)	½
1 cup	packed parsley (leaves and stems)	250 mL
6	leaves kale	6
1 tsp	Ginger Juice (page 24) or 1 tbsp (15 mL) chopped ginger	5 mL
½	lemon, peeled	½
8	stalks celery	8

Preparation: 5 to 10 minutes
Equipment: juice extractor
Makes 2 portions

1. Run all ingredients through juice extractor.

TIPS

For a sweeter, slightly less green juice, add 1 apple.

Keeps 1 day in the refrigerator in an airtight container.

Absolute Juice

2	apples	2
1	bulb fennel (with leaves)	1
1	large pink grapefruit	1
4	stalks celery	4

Preparation: 5 to 10 minutes
Equipment: juice extractor or centrifuge
Makes 2 portions

1. Run all ingredients through juice extractor or centrifuge.

TIP

Keeps 2 days in the refrigerator in an airtight container.

Hippocrates Juice

3 cups	green pea shoots	750 mL
½ cup	packed fresh cilantro (leaves and stems)	125 mL
1 cup	cucumber with skin	250 mL
10	stalks celery	10
½	lemon, peeled	½

Preparation: 5 to 10 minutes
Equipment: juice extractor

Makes 2 portions

1. Run all ingredients through juice extractor.

TIPS

For a sweeter, less green juice, add 1 apple.

Keeps 1 day in the refrigerator in an airtight container.

Red Lips Juice

2	apples	2
1	large red beet	1
6	carrots	6
2 tsp	Ginger Juice (page 24) or 2 tbsp (30 mL) chopped ginger	10 mL

Preparation: 5 to 10 minutes
Equipment: juice extractor or centrifuge

Makes 2 portions

1. Run all ingredients through centrifuge or juice extractor.

TIP

Keeps 2 days in the refrigerator in an airtight container.

Inner Jazz Elixir

2 tsp	spirulina or 2 to 4 tbsp (30 to 60 mL) wheat grass juice	10 mL
1	banana	1
2/3 cup	chopped pineapple pieces	150 mL
2/3 cup	mango flesh	150 mL
1	orange, peeled, external membrane removed	1
1 1/2 cups	water	375 mL
1/2 tsp	chopped ginger	2 mL
30	drops ginseng tincture (optional)	30

Preparation: 10 minutes

Equipment: blender

Makes 2 portions

1. In blender, combine all ingredients and blend to a smoothie.

TIPS

To drink chilled, use frozen fruits or replace some of the water with ice cubes.

Keeps 2 days in the refrigerator in an airtight container.

Supreme Fruit Smoothie

1 tbsp	melted coconut oil	15 mL
3	grapefruit segments	3
4	strawberries, trimmed	4
3/4 cup	mango flesh	175 mL
1/2 cup	raspberries	125 mL
1/2 tsp	ground cardamom	2 mL
3 tbsp	Date Paste (page 25) or 3 seedless dates	45 mL
1 1/2 cups	water	375 mL

Preparation: 5 minutes

Equipment: blender

Makes 2 portions

1. In blender, combine all ingredients and blend into a thick smoothie.

TIP

Keeps 2 days in the refrigerator in an airtight container.

Beebuzz Elixir

1/2 cup	unpeeled almonds	125 mL
2 1/2 cups	water	625 mL
3	bananas	3
1 tsp	ground turmeric	5 mL
1 tsp	mesquite powder	5 mL
1 tsp	lucuma powder	5 mL
1/4 tsp	ground cinnamon	1 mL
1/8 tsp	ground cayenne pepper	0.5 mL
1 tsp	freshly squeezed lemon juice	5 mL
1/2 tsp	alcohol-free vanilla essence	2 mL
2 tsp	honey (preferably organic and non-pasteurized)	10 mL
1 tbsp	bee pollen	15 mL
14	drops ginkgo biloba tincture (optional)	14

Soaking: 8 hours
Preparation: 15 minutes
Equipment: blender and filter

Makes 2 portions

1. *Soaking:* In a bowl, soak almonds in water to cover for 8 hours. Rinse thoroughly and discard soaking water.

2. Make a milk with almonds and water (see page 28).

3. In blender, combine milk and remaining ingredients and blend into a thick smoothie.

TIPS

To drink chilled, use frozen fruits or replace some of the water with ice cubes.

Keeps 2 days in the refrigerator in an airtight container.

Peach Lhassi

2 cups	Nut Yogurt (page 135)	500 mL
	Flesh of 2 peaches	
2 tbsp	agave nectar	30 mL
¼ tsp	ground cardamom	1 mL
1 cup	water	250 mL

Preparation: 5 minutes
Equipment: blender

Makes 2 portions

1. In blender, combine all ingredients and blend to a creamy beverage.

TIP

Keeps 2 days in the refrigerator in an airtight container.

Nourishing Tisane

| 7 cups | boiling water (see Tips, below) | 1.75 L |
| 1 cup | dried nettles or 2 to 3 cups (500 to 750 mL) fresh nettles (see Tips, below) | 250 mL |

Soaking: 6 to 12 hours
Preparation: 5 minutes

Makes 8 cups (2 L)

1. *Soaking:* In an 8-cup (2 L) container, pour boiling water on the herbs. Steep overnight (6 to 12 hours). Filter.

2. Use this tisane cold as a liquid in the preparation of milks and smoothies.

TIPS

To ensure that the water is below 105°F (41°C) and won't destroy any of the enzymes in the ingredients, after bringing water to a boil, set aside to cool slightly, for 2 to 3 minutes.

For the fresh nettles, you can replace or add the same quantities of other herbs like horsetail, oat, red clover or any other nutritional herbs that are not contraindicated when combined.

Keeps 5 days in the refrigerator in an airtight container.

Kombu Mojito

1 1/2 cups	chopped pineapple	375 mL
8	medium-size mint leaves	8
	Juice of half a lemon	
1 tbsp	agave nectar	15 mL
1/4 cup	water	60 mL
1 cup	Kombucha (page 128)	250 mL

Preparation: 5 minutes
Equipment: blender

Makes 2 portions

1. In blender, combine all ingredients except kombucha and blend to a juice with a smooth, consistent texture.

2. Pour into glasses, then add kombucha.

TIP

Keeps 2 days in the refrigerator in an airtight container.

Hot Chocolate

1/4 cup	cocoa powder	60 mL
1/4 cup	coconut butter	60 mL
4 tbsp	Date Paste (page 25) or 4 seedless dates	60 mL
1/4 cup	cashew nuts	60 mL
2 cups	warm filtered water (see Tips, below)	500 mL

To make spicy hot chocolate, add:

1/8 tsp	ground cayenne pepper	0.5 mL
1/8 tsp	ground ginger	0.5 mL
1/8 tsp	ground cinnamon	0.5 mL
1/8 tsp	ground anise	0.5 mL
1/8 tsp	ground cloves	0.5 mL

Or

To make almond hot chocolate, add:

1/8 tsp	almond essence	0.5 mL

Preparation: 5 minutes
Equipment: blender

Makes 2 portions

1. In blender, combine all ingredients and blend to a creamy beverage.

TIPS

For the hot water in this recipe, to ensure that the water is below 105°F (41°C) and won't destroy any of the enzymes in the ingredients, bring water to a boil and set aside to cool slightly, for 2 to 3 minutes.

Keeps 2 days in the refrigerator in an airtight container.

Appetizers

Beet Ravioli

1	large red beet	1

Marinade

1 tbsp	sunflower oil	15 mL
1 tbsp	freshly squeezed lemon juice	15 mL
1/4 tsp	sea salt	1 mL

Mango and Sweet Potato Filling

1/3 cup	chopped mango	75 mL
1/3	medium sweet potato, peeled	1/3
3/4 tsp	psyllium	3 mL
1/8 tsp	nutritional yeast	0.5 mL
1/8 tsp	onion powder	0.5 mL
1/8 tsp	sea salt	0.5 mL
1/8 tsp	ground nutmeg	0.5 mL
	Balsamic Raspberry Dressing (see below)	

Preparation: 30 minutes
Marinating: 4 hours
Equipment: food processor, mandoline

Makes 10 ravioli
4 appetizers or 2 main dishes

1. Using a mandoline, cut beet into 20 very thin round large slices. Place in a container of water and let soak for 2 hours.

2. *Marinade:* Using a whisk, blend marinade ingredients. Drain beets and pour over top. Let marinate for 2 hours.

3. *Mango and Sweet Potato Filling:* In food processor, purée filling ingredients to an even consistency.

4. Once beets have marinated, assemble ravioli. On a slice of beet, place 1 tbsp (15 mL) of filling, then cover with another slice of beet and pinch edges.

5. Top with Balsamic Raspberry Dressing before serving. Serve cold.

TIP

Beets can also be filled with Macadamia Ricotta Cheese (page 117).

Balsamic Raspberry Dressing

1 cup	packed raspberries	250 mL
1 cup	olive oil	250 mL
1/2 cup	balsamic vinegar	125 mL
1/4 cup	water	60 mL
1/2	clove garlic or 1/2 tsp (2 mL) Garlic Purée (page 25)	1/2
3/4 tsp	sea salt	3 mL
1/2 tsp	ground black pepper	2 mL

Preparation: 10 minutes
Equipment: blender

Makes about 2 cups (500 mL)

1. In blender, combine all ingredients and blend to a dressing of even consistency.

TIP

Keeps 1 week in the refrigerator in an airtight container.

Curry Sushi

2	sheets nori	2
1/2	recipe Curry Paste (see below)	1/2
2	large lettuce leaves	2
1	medium carrot, grated	1
1/4 cup	julienned zucchini	60 mL
1 tbsp	very thinly slivered onion, almost transparent	15 mL
1/4	apple, julienned and sprinkled with lemon juice to prevent darkening	1/4
1/2	avocado, sliced	1/2
1/2 cup	packed alfalfa or clover sprouts	125 mL

Preparation: 15 minutes
Equipment: mandoline

TIP

If sushi rolls are to be cut into pieces they must be tighter and smaller. In this case, put a little less carrot and filling inside.

Makes 2 sushi rolls or 16 pieces
4 appetizers or 2 main dishes

1. Lay a sheet of nori on work surface, veined side up and shiny side down. Place 1/4 cup (60 mL) of Curry Paste on top. Using a spatula, spread paste across entire width and along two thirds of length.

2. Take a large lettuce leaf and crush veins by hand (to prevent lettuce from tearing nori during rolling), then lay it on top of the paste. Allow lettuce to extend slightly beyond the edge.

3. Across lettuce leaf, lay alternating rows of grated carrot, zucchini, onion, apple and 3 slices of avocado. Cover with a large handful of alfalfa sprouts. Let filling extend beyond edges so that sushi rolls have attractive ends.

4. Dip fingers in a bowl of water and moisten end of nori that has no paste on it. Roll sushi starting at the other end, keeping roll as tight as possible. Seal roll at end that has been moistened with water. Place roll with seam side down for 1 to 2 minutes to give it time to dry.

5. Cut sushi rolls in half to make "sandwiches" or 8 uniform pieces. Repeat with remaining ingredients. Serve cold.

Curry Paste

2/3 cup	sunflower seeds	150 mL
1 tbsp	Date Paste (page 24) or 1 1/2 seedless dates	15 mL
1 tbsp	water	15 mL
2 tsp	apple cider vinegar	10 mL
1/2 tsp	sunflower oil	2 mL
2 tsp	curry powder	10 mL
1 tsp	Garlic Purée (page 25) or 1 clove garlic	5 mL
1 tsp	each turmeric and cumin	5 mL
1/2 tsp	sea salt	2 mL
1/8 tsp	ground cayenne pepper	0.5 mL
2 tbsp	ground sunflower seeds	30 mL

Soaking: 8 hours
Preparation: 20 minutes
Equipment: food processor

Makes about 1 cup (250 mL)

1. *Soaking:* In a bowl, soak sunflower seeds in water to cover for 8 hours. Rinse thoroughly and discard soaking water.

2. In food processor, combine all ingredients except ground sunflower seeds and blend until mixture is creamy and smooth.

3. Add ground sunflower seeds and blend again for 1 minute.

TIP

Keeps 7 days in the refrigerator in an airtight container.

Veggie-Spread Spring Rolls

2	sheets rice paper	2
5	large lettuce leaves	5
1	medium carrot, grated	1
1/4 cup	julienned zucchini	60 mL
1 tbsp	very thinly slivered onion, almost transparent	15 mL
1/4 cup	slivered red cabbage	60 mL
1/4	recipe Veggie-Spread (see right)	1/4
1/2 cup	packed clover sprouts	125 mL
	Poppy seeds or black sesame seeds (optional)	

Preparation: 15 minutes
Equipment: mandoline

TIPS

Serve with Tibet Fat-Free Dressing (see below), if desired.

If sushi rolls are to be cut into pieces they must be tighter and smaller. In this case, put a little less filling inside.

Makes 2 rolls or 16 pieces
4 appetizers or 2 main dishes

1. In a bowl of warm water, soak rice paper and place on end of table with one end hanging over edge.

2. Take 1 or 2 large lettuce leaves and crush veins by hand (to prevent them from breaking the sheet during rolling), then lay them over half the length and three quarters of the width of the rice paper. They should not overlap, but fill entire surface.

3. Across lettuce leaf, place alternating rows of grated carrot, zucchini, onion and red cabbage. Place 1/4 cup (60 mL) of Veggie Spread on top and spread mixture across lettuce leaf. Top with a handful of sprouts then cover all with another large leaf of lettuce whose veins have been crushed. It is important that the rice paper sheet be kept separate from its filling by a layer of lettuce to prevent the rice paper from tearing. Sprinkle top part of rice sheet with poppy seeds or black sesame seeds, if using.

4. To roll, pick up end that hangs over edge of table and pull it over the filling. Tamp down with hand to eliminate empty space. Fold up sides, then roll up sheet, using slight pressure toward the top to tighten it. Cut rolls to make "sandwiches" or 8 pieces. Repeat with remaining ingredients. Serve cold.

Tibet Fat-Free Dressing

1 1/4 cups	water	300 mL
1/2 cup	lemon juice	125 mL
1/4 cup	nama shoyu or wheat-free tamari sauce	60 mL
3 tbsp	chopped ginger or 1 tbsp (15 mL) Ginger Juice (page 24)	45 mL
1 1/2	clove garlic or 1 1/2 tsp (7 mL) Garlic Purée (page 25)	1 1/2
1/4 cup	agave nectar	60 mL
1 1/2 tsp	each sea salt and curry powder	7 mL
1/8 tsp	ground cayenne pepper	0.5 mL

Preparation: 10 minutes
Equipment: blender

Makes about 2 cups (500 mL)

1. In blender, combine all ingredients and blend to a liquid sauce of even consistency.

TIPS

Keeps 2 weeks in the refrigerator in an airtight container.

This sauce keeps several months if it is prepared without water and water is added just before serving. Always blend thoroughly before using.

Veggie Spread

³/₄ cup	sunflower seeds	175 mL
¹/₂ cup	coarsely chopped carrot	125 mL
1¹/₂ tbsp	coarsely chopped red onion	22 mL
2 tbsp	coarsely chopped packed fresh parsley (leaves and stems)	30 mL
2 tbsp	sunflower oil	30 mL
1¹/₂ tbsp	apple cider vinegar	22 mL
1 tbsp	freshly squeezed lemon juice	15 mL
1 tbsp	Ginger Juice (page 24) or 1 tbsp (15 mL) chopped ginger	15 mL
1 tsp	cumin seeds, ground	5 mL
1 tsp	Garlic Purée (page 25) or 1 small clove garlic	5 mL
¹/₂ tsp	sea salt	2 mL
¹/₄ cup	ground sesame seeds	60 mL
1 tbsp	nutritional yeast	15 mL

Soaking: 8 hours
Preparation: 20 minutes
Equipment: food processor

Makes about 1¹/₂ cups (375 mL)

1. In a bowl, soak sunflower seeds in water for 8 hours. Rinse thoroughly and discard soaking water.

2. In food processor, combine all ingredients except ground sesame seeds and yeast and blend until mixture is creamy and smooth.

3. Add ground sesame seeds and yeast. Blend again for 1 minute to incorporate.

TIP

Keeps 5 days in the refrigerator in an airtight container.

Mushroom Caps

30	white mushrooms, about 1 inch (2.5 cm) in diameter	30
1/2	recipe Country Spread (page 120)	1/2
5 tbsp	crème fraîche (optional)	75 mL
3 tbsp	finely chopped parsley	45 mL
2 tbsp	shelled hemp seeds	30 mL

Preparation: 15 minutes
Marinating: 30 minutes
Dehydration: 1 hour
Equipment: dehydrator

Makes 30 mushrooms
6 appetizers or 3 main dishes

1. Trim mushrooms and place caps in Mushroom Marinade (see below) for 30 minutes. Use stems to prepare Country Spread recipe.
2. With a pastry bag (or spoon), stuff marinated mushroom caps with a large ball, about 1 1/2 tbsp (22 mL), of Country Spread.
3. Place in dehydrator at 105°F (41°C) for about 1 hour. Spread should harden slightly on the outside but mushrooms should remain juicy.
4. Before serving, garnish with 1/2 tsp (2 mL) crème fraîche, if using, and sprinkle with chopped parsley and shelled hemp seeds.

TIPS

For variety, prepare same recipe with 4 large portobello mushrooms.

Keeps 4 days in the refrigerator in an airtight container.

Mushroom Marinade

1/2 cup	wheat-free tamari sauce	125 mL
1 1/2	cloves garlic, chopped or 1 1/2 tsp (7 mL) Garlic Purée (page 25)	1 1/2
1 cup	water	250 mL
1 1/2 tsp	dried thyme	7 mL
1/2 tsp	ground black pepper	2 mL

Makes 2 cups (500 mL)

1. In a bowl, using a whisk, blend all ingredients together.

TIPS

This marinade can be used for other mushrooms or vegetables.

Keeps 1 month in the refrigerator in an airtight container.

Olivetta Bruschetta

⅓	recipe Kalamata Olive Tapenade (page 116)	⅓
20	Onion Bread triangles (page 142)	20
3 tbsp	Cashew Nut Cheese (page 125)	45 mL
	Mixed Salad (see below)	

Preparation: 5 minutes

Makes 20 bruschettas
4 appetizers or 2 main dishes

1. Spread 1 to 2 tsp (5 to 10 mL) of tapenade on each onion triangle.
2. With a pastry bag or a clean ketchup bottle, top each bruschetta with 1 tsp (5 mL) Cashew Nut Cheese.
3. Top with mixed salad.

Mixed Salad

1 tbsp	slivered onion	15 mL
½	red or yellow bell pepper, cut into very small cubes	½
¼	tomato, cut into small cubes	¼
¼ tsp	dried or fresh thyme	1 mL
⅛ tsp	sea salt	0.5 mL
⅛ tsp	ground black pepper	0.5 mL
⅛ tsp	dried or fresh sage	0.5 mL

1. In a salad bowl, blend all ingredients. Let stand for 15 to 30 minutes.
2. Before serving, discard water that has formed in bottom of bowl. Serve cold.

Ricotta Roulade

³/₄ cup	Macadamia Ricotta Cheese (page 117)	175 mL
1	large zucchini	1
¼	red bell pepper, cut into 25 very thin sticks	¼
1 cup	clover or alfalfa sprouts	250 mL

Preparation: 10 minutes
Equipment: mandoline

Makes 25 rolls
6 appetizers or 3 main dishes

1. Using mandoline, slice zucchini lengthwise into 25 very thin pieces.

2. Spread zucchini slices on work surface. Place 1¹/₂ tsp (7 mL) of Macadamia Ricotta Cheese on one end of each slice. Place 1 stick of bell pepper on top of ricotta, allowing it to slightly extend past the edge of the zucchini slice. Place a pinch of sprouts on top.

3. Roll up each slice starting at the end with the filling. Hold roll in place with a toothpick, if necessary. Arrange rolls on a tray. Serve cold.

Cheese Roll

8	Cheese Slices (see below)	8
1 cup	Country Spread (page 120)	250 mL
½ cup	tightly packed sprouted sunflower seeds	125 mL

Vegetables (see Tip, right)

½	medium carrot, julienned	½
⅕	medium zucchini, julienned	⅕
½ cup	slivered red cabbage	125 mL

Preparation: 5 minutes

Makes 8 rolls as appetizers or 2 main dishes

1. Lay cheese slices on work surface.

2. Using a spatula, spread 2 tbsp (30 mL) of Country Spread across the entire width and two thirds up each slice.

3. Cover the width with sunflower seed sprouts. On top of this, add a line of carrot, then a line of zucchini, and then a line of red cabbage.

4. Roll up the cheese slices lengthwise. Hold in place with toothpicks, if necessary. Serve cold.

TIP

Vegetables can be replaced by any other vegetables of your choice.

Cheese Slices

1 cup	cashew nuts	250 mL
1 cup	coarsely chopped red bell pepper	250 mL
¼	butternut squash, diced	¼
6 tbsp	water	90 mL
2 tbsp	lemon juice	30 mL
4 tsp	wheat-free tamari sauce	20 mL
4 tsp	olive oil	20 mL
2 tsp	finely chopped jalapeño pepper	10 mL
2 tsp	Garlic Purée (page 25) or 2 cloves garlic, chopped	10 mL
2 tbsp	nutritional yeast	30 mL
2 tbsp	sea salt	30 mL
2 tsp	psyllium	10 mL

Soaking: 4 hours
Preparation: 20 minutes
Dehydration: about 10 hours
Equipment: blender, dehydrator

Makes 18 slices

1. *Soaking:* In a bowl, soak cashew nuts in water to cover for 4 hours. Rinse thoroughly, then drain and discard soaking water.

2. In blender, combine all ingredients except psyllium and blend to a uniformly creamy sauce.

3. Add psyllium, then blend for several seconds to mix it in thoroughly.

4. Pour mixture into a bowl. Let stand for 10 minutes to give the psyllium time to form mucilage.

5. Spread 2 cups (500 mL) of the mixture on a nonstick dehydrator sheet, leaving a border. Even out with a spatula, preferably an angled one.

6. With a butter knife or spatula, trace lines across the sheet to make nine 3-inch (7.5 cm) squares.

7. Repeat the procedure with the remaining mixture.

8. Place in dehydrator set at 105°F (41°C) for 10 hours. The cheese slices are ready when they can be separated without breaking and are no longer sticky to the touch.

TIP

Keeps 2 weeks in the refrigerator in an airtight container.

Pesto Tagliatelle

2	medium zucchini, trimmed	2
¼ cup	Pistachio Basil Pesto (page 121) or 20 medium basil leaves, slivered (for a lighter recipe)	60 mL
½ tsp	sea salt	2 mL
½ tsp	Garlic Purée (page 25) or ½ clove garlic, chopped	2 mL
1 tbsp	olive oil	15 mL
6	kalamata olives, pitted, chopped	6
2 tbsp	pine nuts	30 mL

Preparation: 10 minutes

Equipment: mandoline or vegetable peeler

Makes 4 appetizers or 2 main dishes

1. Using a mandoline or vegetable peeler, cut zucchini into long thin strips, then julienne strips into long tagliatelle.

2. In a salad bowl, combine zucchini tagliatelle with pesto, salt, garlic and olive oil.

3. Place tagliatelli in dishes and top with chopped olives and pine nuts. Serve cold.

GOOD AND BAD FATS

We divide the large family of fats into three categories: saturated fatty acids, monounsaturates and polyunsaturates. All fat is made up of chains of carbon atoms of different lengths, surrounded by hydrogen atoms. The more hydrogen atoms there are in a fat, the more saturated it is.

All oil, or natural fat, contains the three categories of saturation in varying degrees. For example, olive oil, which is monounsaturated, contains a predominance of monounsaturated chains, but also saturated and polyunsaturated fats. It is essential to consume the three families of fat, because they all play a different role in the body.

The shorter the chain, the less energy the body needs for digesting it. On the other hand, the lower the level of saturation, as in the case of hemp or flax seed oils, the more likely the fatty acids are to be altered by heat and to develop free radicals.

We therefore recommend consuming polyunsaturated fatty acids in their original form, as in whole hemp seeds or chia seeds. Although they are less fragile, monounsaturated fats are often found already altered and rancid on supermarket shelves. Here again, it is better to consume them in their complete form, by eating avocados, olives, sunflower seeds, almonds and nuts in general.

Cooking monounsaturated and polyunsaturated fats inevitably leads to the formation of free radicals. The purest olive oil becomes a poison after being cooked too long! That is why, in this case, we recommend using a saturated fat with medium-length chains of fatty acids, such as coconut oil. It is a masterpiece of nature for the human body. Containing 8 to 12 carbon atoms, it can be quickly transformed into glycogen or proteins, making it a powerful fuel for athletes.

Cauliflower Nigiri Sushi

Cauliflower Rice

1	medium cauliflower	1
2 tsp	rice vinegar	10 mL
2 tsp	psyllium	10 mL
1 tsp	sea salt	5 mL
1/8 tsp	ground black pepper	0.5 mL
1/2	very ripe mango	1/2
1/2	very ripe avocado	1/2
1	sheet nori	1
20	raspberries	20

Preparation: 15 minutes
Equipment: food processor

Makes 10 nigiri
4 appetizers or 2 main dishes

1. *Cauliflower Rice:* In a food processor, combine all ingredients and chop into small pieces the size of grains of rice. Let stand 15 minutes.

2. Divide mixture into 10 balls. In the palm of your hand, form balls into small rectangular mounds about 3 inches (7.5 cm) long, 1 inch (2.5 cm) wide and 1 1/2 inches (4 cm) thick.

3. Using a spoon, remove pits from mango and avocado. Cut fruit into large slices about 3 inches (7.5 cm) long, 1 inch (2.5 cm) wide and 3/4 inch (2 cm) thick.

4. Place a piece of mango or avocado on each cauliflower rice mound.

5. With scissors, cut 10 strips of nori measuring 2 1/4 by 1/2 inch (6 by 1 cm)

6. Place each nigiri lengthwise centered on a strip of nori. Moisten both ends of each strip with water and glue them together on the top of the sushi.

7. With a fork, lightly crush raspberries to separate them into small seeds. Place raspberry "caviar" on top of the nigiri. Serve cold.

TIP

Rice keeps 4 days in the refrigerator in an airtight container.

Stuffed Endives

Mango Chutney

1 cup	cubed mango	250 mL
1/2	zucchini, cut into small cubes (approx.)	1/2
1/2 cup	finely chopped red bell pepper	125 mL
1/2 cup	finely chopped packed fresh cilantro (leaves and stems)	125 mL
1/4 cup	finely chopped red onion	60 mL
2 tbsp	freshly squeezed lemon juice	30 mL
1/2 tsp	sea salt	2 mL
1/4 tsp	finely chopped jalapeño pepper	1 mL
1/8 tsp	ground cayenne pepper	0.5 mL
8	large endive leaves	8

Topping

Hemp Sauce (see below)

Preparation: 15 minutes

Makes 8 stuffed endives
4 appetizers or 2 main dishes

1. *Mango Chutney:* In a large bowl, blend together all ingredients.
2. Top each endive leaf with about 1/4 cup (60 mL) of chutney.
3. Garnish with lines of Hemp Sauce. Serve cold.

Hemp Sauce

1/2 cup	shelled hemp seeds	125 mL
1 1/2 cups	cauliflower	375 mL
3/4 cup	water	175 mL
1/2 cup	sunflower oil	125 mL
1/2 cup	olive oil	125 mL
1/4 cup	freshly squeezed lemon juice	60 mL
2 tbsp	apple cider vinegar	30 mL
1 tbsp	fresh chives	15 mL
2 tsp	nutritional yeast	10 mL
1 tsp	sea salt	5 mL
1/4 tsp	ground black pepper	1 mL

Preparation: 10 minutes
Equipment: blender

Makes 2 1/2 cups (625 mL)

1. In a blender, combine all ingredients and blend to a sauce of even consistency.

TIP
Keeps 5 days in the refrigerator in an airtight container.

Pesto Bombs

4	medium tomatoes	4
½ cup	Pistachio Basil Pesto (page 121)	125 mL
2 tbsp	olive oil	30 mL
2 tbsp	Caper Aïoli (page 166) (optional)	30 mL
1 cup	arugula	250 mL
1 cup	sunflower sprouts	250 mL
¼ cup	capers	60 mL
¼ cup	Croutons (page 93)	60 mL

Preparation: 15 minutes

Makes 4 appetizers or 2 main dishes

1. Cut "hat" off tomatoes and set aside. Scoop out flesh from tomatoes and save for another recipe.

2. In a bowl, blend together Pistachio Basil Pesto, olive oil and aïoli, if using. Fill tomatoes with mixture.

3. Add arugula and sunflower sprouts to tomatoes. Top with capers and croutons. Replace tomato "hats" before serving. Serve cold.

Lettuga Tacos

4	large lettuce or collard green leaves	4
¾ cup	Oaxaca Spread (page 118)	175 mL
1	avocado, sliced	1
½	red bell pepper, julienned	½
½ cup	corn kernels (about 1 ear of corn)	125 mL
⅓ cup	finely chopped leek	75 mL
4	stems fresh cilantro	4
1 tsp	chili powder	5 mL

Preparation: 5 minutes

Makes 4 tacos
4 appetizers or 2 main dishes

1. In center of each leaf of lettuce, spread 3 tbsp (45 mL) of Oaxaca Spread over entire length of lettuce.

2. Place avocado slices, julienned red pepper, 2 tbsp (30 mL) of corn, a line of chopped leek and a stem of cilantro on top. Sprinkle with chili powder.

3. Serve as is on dishes and roll up to eat. Serve cold.

Tomato Guacamole Towers

2	medium tomatoes	2

Corn and Avocado Tartare

2 to 3	avocados, cut into small cubes	2 to 3
1/2 cup	corn kernels (about 1 ear of corn)	125 mL
2 tbsp	chopped sun-dried tomatoes	30 mL
2 tbsp	finely chopped packed fresh cilantro (leaves and stems)	30 mL
1/2	stalk celery, diced	1/2
1/2 tsp	chili powder	2 mL
1/8 tsp	sea salt	0.5 mL
1/8 tsp	ground cumin	0.5 mL
	Zest and juice of 1 lime	
2 cups	arugula shoots	500 mL

Preparation: 10 minutes
Equipment: round cookie cutter

Makes 4 appetizers or 2 main dishes

1. Dice tomatoes and drain surplus liquid. Set aside.

2. *Corn and Avocado Tartare:* In a bowl, combine all ingredients and gently blend.

3. Place cookie cutter in the center of a serving dish. Surround it with a ring of arugula shoots.

4. Place 3 tbsp (45 mL) of tartare inside cookie cutter. Using the back of a spoon, pack down mixture without crushing it. Place 3 tbsp (45 mL) of tomatoes on top, then 2 tbsp (30 mL) more of tartare. Top with 2 tbsp (30 mL) of tomatoes and pack down with back of spoon to form a tower that is compact but not crushed.

5. Repeat procedure for three more dishes. Serve cold.

Soups

Spinach Pistachio Cream Soup

2 cups	water, divided	500 mL
2½ cups	spinach	625 mL
½	avocado	½
¼	lime	¼
½ cup	chopped fresh cilantro (leaves and stems)	125 mL
¼ cup	pistachio nuts	60 mL
1 tsp	sea salt	5 mL

Optional

For each 1-cup (250 mL) portion, add:

1 tsp	Crème Fraîche (page 175)	5 mL

Preparation: 10 minutes
Equipment: blender

Makes 4 portions

1. In blender, combine half the water and all other ingredients and blend into a thick, smooth paste.

2. Add remaining water and blend to obtain a creamy soup. Garnish with Crème Fraîche, if desired.

TIPS

To eat this soup hot, replace cold water with hot water (see Tips, page 71).

Keeps 3 days in the refrigerator in an airtight container.

Cream of Tomato Soup

1½ cups	water, divided	375 mL
1½ cups	chopped tomatoes	375 mL
1¼ cups	chopped carrots	300 mL
½ cup	cashew nuts	125 mL
1 tbsp	chopped fresh cilantro (leaves and stems)	15 mL
1½ tsp	freshly squeezed lemon juice	7 mL
1½ tsp	sea salt	7 mL
1 tsp	chili powder	5 mL

Preparation: 15 minutes
Equipment: blender

Makes 4 portions

1. In blender, combine half the water and all other ingredients and blend into a thick, smooth paste.

2. Add remaining water and blend to obtain a creamy soup.

TIPS

To eat this soup hot, replace cold water with hot water (see Tips, page 71).

Keeps 3 days in the refrigerator in an airtight container.

Carrot Curry Soup

1/2 cup	carrot juice (about 5 carrots)	125 mL
1 cup	apple juice (about 3 apples)	250 mL
1/2	lemon, peeled, outer white membrane removed	1/2
3/4 tsp	ginger or 1/4 tsp (1 mL) Ginger Juice (page 24)	3 mL
3/4 cup	chopped peeled carrot	175 mL
1/2 cup	water	125 mL
3/4 cup	cashew nuts	175 mL
2 tsp	curry powder	10 mL
1 tsp	sea salt	5 mL

Preparation: 20 minutes

Equipment: blender, juice extractor or centrifuge

Makes 4 portions

1. If needed, run carrots, apples, lemon and ginger through juice extractor or centrifuge to obtain desired quantities of juice.

2. In blender, combine 3/4 cup (175 mL) chopped carrot and water and blend to a purée.

3. Add carrot, apple, lemon and ginger juices and remaining ingredients to blender, then reduce to a soup of even consistency.

TIPS

To serve this soup hot, replace cold water with hot water (see Tips, page 71).

Keeps 3 days in the refrigerator in an airtight container.

Onion Soup

1	recipe Onion Confit (see below)	1

Broth

1/4 cup	miso	60 mL
1/4 cup	wheat-free tamari sauce	60 mL
3 1/2 cups	hot filtered or spring water, divided (see Tips, right)	875 mL

Optional

2 tsp	red wine	10 mL
4	Croutons (page 93)	4

Preparation: 5 minutes

Makes 4 portions

1. Divide Onion Confit into 4 soup bowls.
2. *Broth:* In a large bowl, using a whisk, dilute miso and tamari sauce in 1 cup (250 mL) of hot water.
3. Add remaining water, then red wine, if using, and mix again.
4. Pour broth into soup bowls. Top with croutons, if using.

TIPS

To ensure that the hot water used in this recipe is below 105°F (41°C) and won't destroy any of the enzymes in the ingredients, bring water to a boil and set aside to cool slightly, for 2 to 3 minutes.

Keeps 1 week in the refrigerator in an airtight container.

Onion Confit for Onion Soup

2 1/2 cups	slivered onions (see Tips, right)	625 mL
1 tbsp	wheat-free tamari sauce	15 mL
3/4 tsp	sunflower oil	3 mL
2 tsp	ground thyme	10 mL
1/2 tsp	chili powder	2 mL
1/4 tsp	ground pepper	1 mL

Preparation: 20 minutes
Dehydration: 3 hours
Equipment: dehydrator, food processor or mandoline

Makes 4 portions

1. In a salad bowl, combine onions and remaining ingredients by hand.
2. Spread on trays and place in dehydrator at 105°F (41°C) for 3 hours.

TIPS

Use food processor or mandoline to cut onions into slivers.

Keeps 1 month in the refrigerator in an airtight container.

Miso Soup

| 1 | recipe Miso Soup Broth (see below) | 1 |
| 4 cups | hot filtered or spring water (see Tips, left) | 1 L |

Mixture

¼ cup	goji berries	60 mL
4	large white mushrooms, sliced	4
½	green onion, slivered	½
¼ cup	small pieces wakame or arame	60 mL

Preparation: 10 minutes
Equipment: blender

Makes 2 main courses or 4 appetizers

1. In a large container, pour broth. Add hot water and blend with a whisk.
2. Divide mixture among soup bowls. Pour broth equally on top.

TIPS

To ensure that the hot water used in this recipe is below 105°F (41°C) and won't destroy any of the enzymes in the ingredients, bring water to a boil and set aside to cool slightly, for 2 to 3 minutes.

Keeps 5 to 7 days in refrigerator in two separate, airtight containers (1 for vegetables and 1 for broth).

Miso Soup Broth

¼ cup	miso	60 mL
¼ cup	wheat-free tamari sauce	60 mL
1 tsp	Ginger Juice (page 24) or 2 tsp (10 mL) chopped ginger	5 mL

1. In blender, combine all ingredients.

Raw Borscht

1	medium beet, shredded	1

Broth

½	medium beet, cut into cubes	½
1	tomato, coarsely chopped	1
¼ cup	sun-dried tomatoes	60 mL
2 tbsp	coarsely chopped fresh dill	30 mL
3 cups	water	750 mL
¼ cup	coarsely chopped red onion	60 mL
2 tbsp	olive oil	30 mL
1 tbsp	freshly squeezed lemon juice	15 mL
1 tbsp	agave nectar	15 mL
⅛ tsp	ground cloves	0.5 mL

Optional

¼ cup	Crème Fraîche (page 175) or Nut Yogurt (page 135)	60 mL

Preparation: 25 minutes
Equipment: blender

Makes 4 portions

1. Divide shredded beet into 4 soup bowls.
2. *Broth:* In blender, combine all ingredients and blend to an evenly consistent soup with no pieces. Pour into bowls.
3. Garnish with Crème Fraîche or Nut Yogurt, if desired.

TIP

Keeps 3 days in the refrigerator in an airtight container.

Cream of Mushroom Soup

2 3/4 cups	water, divided	675 mL
2 1/2 cups	white mushrooms	625 mL
3 tbsp	sliced red onion	45 mL
2 tbsp	freshly squeezed lemon juice	30 mL
1 tbsp	miso	15 mL
1 tbsp	wheat-free tamari sauce	15 mL
1 cup	cashew nuts	250 mL
1 tsp	sea salt	5 mL
1 tbsp	dried rosemary	15 mL

Preparation: 10 minutes
Equipment: blender

Makes 4 portions

1. In blender, combine half the water and all other ingredients except rosemary and blend into a thick, smooth paste.

2. Add remaining water and blend to obtain a creamy soup.

3. Add rosemary, then blend briefly to incorporate it into the soup while retaining small pieces.

TIPS

To serve this soup hot, replace cold water with hot water (see Tips, page 71).

Keeps 5 to 7 days in the refrigerator in an airtight container.

Tonkinese Soup

Vegetable Mixture

1	medium zucchini, cut into spaghetti (see Tips, right)	1
1/2 cup	grated carrot	125 mL
2 tbsp	chopped green onion	30 mL
1/2 cup	chopped fresh cilantro	125 mL
4	slices lime (optional)	4

Broth

1 tsp	ground cumin	5 mL
	Juice of 1/2 lemon	
1/3 cup	wheat-free tamari sauce	75 mL
1/2 tsp	Garlic Purée (page 25) or 1/2 clove garlic, finely chopped	2 mL
2 1/2 tbsp	agave nectar	37 mL
1 tsp	sea salt	5 mL
3/4 tsp	curry powder	3 mL
1/8 tsp	ground cayenne pepper	0.5 mL
1 tsp	Ginger Juice (page 24) or 1 tbsp (15 mL) finely chopped ginger	5 mL
4 cups	hot filtered or spring water (see Tips, page 79)	1 L

Preparation: 25 minutes

Equipment: blender, spiral cut machine or mandoline

Makes 4 portions

1. *Vegetable Mixture:* Prepare vegetables and set aside.

2. *Broth:* In blender or with a whisk, combine all ingredients except water.

3. Pour broth into a large container. Add water and blend with a whisk.

4. Divide vegetables into bowls and pour broth on top.

TIPS

Use a mandoline or spiral cut machine to cut zucchini into spaghetti.

Keeps 4 days in refrigerator in two separate, airtight containers (1 for vegetables and 1 for broth).

Butternut Squash Cilantro Soup

2 cups	water, divided	500 mL
¼	medium butternut squash, coarsely chopped	¼
½ cup	chopped celery	125 mL
¼ cup	chopped onion	60 mL
⅓ cup	chopped red bell pepper	75 mL
½	avocado, coarsely chopped	½
2 tbsp	wheat-free tamari sauce	30 mL
10	branches fresh cilantro (leaves and stems)	10

Preparation: 15 minutes

Equipment: blender

Makes 4 portions

1. In blender, combine half the water and all other ingredients except cilantro and blend into a thick, smooth paste.

2. Add remaining water and blend to obtain a creamy soup.

3. Add cilantro and blend briefly by pulsing to incorporate it into the soup while retaining pieces of leaves.

TIPS

To serve this soup hot, replace cold water with hot water (see Tips, page 71).

Keeps 3 days in the refrigerator in an airtight container.

Kale Soup

5	leaves kale and/or spinach and/or Swiss chard, trimmed and chopped with a knife	5
1	avocado, coarsely chopped	1
1 cup	sunflower or clover sprouts	250 mL
1/4 cup	shelled hemp seeds	60 mL
2 1/2 cups	water or Nourishing Tisane (page 36)	625 mL
1	lemon, peeled with a knife, outer white membrane removed	1
2 tbsp	wheat-free tamari sauce or 1 tbsp (15 mL) nama shoyu	30 mL
1 tsp	ground coriander seeds	5 mL

Preparation: 5 minutes
Equipment: blender

Makes 4 portions

1. In blender, combine all ingredients and blend into a thick, smooth soup.

TIP

Keeps 1 day in the refrigerator in an airtight container.

Gazpacho

3	medium tomatoes, coarsely chopped, divided	3
1/3	red bell pepper, coarsely chopped, divided	1/3
1/4	cucumber, peeled and coarsely chopped, divided	1/4
2 tbsp	chopped red onion, divided	30 mL
1/2	avocado, coarsely chopped	1/2
1/2 cup	water	125 mL
2 tbsp	olive oil	30 mL
1/2 tsp	sea salt	2 mL
1/2 tsp	apple cider vinegar	2 mL
1/2 tsp	maple syrup	2 mL
1/4 tsp	Garlic Purée (page 25) or 1/2 clove garlic	1 mL

Preparation: 10 minutes
Equipment: blender

Makes 4 portions

1. In blender, combine half each of the tomatoes, bell pepper, cucumber and red onion along with remaining ingredients and blend to a creamy, evenly consistent purée.

2. Dice remaining vegetables into very small pieces and add to soup.

TIP
Keeps 2 or 3 days in the refrigerator in an airtight container.

Maelstrom Soup

Vegetables

1 cup	diced zucchini	250 mL
1 cup	diced mushrooms	250 mL
1/2	medium tomato, diced	1/2
3/4 cup	chopped broccoli	175 mL
1/4 cup	diced red onion	60 mL
1 tbsp	fresh or dried tarragon	15 mL
1/2 tsp	finely ground sea salt	2 mL
1/8 tsp	ground black pepper	0.5 mL

Broth

1	lime, peeled with a knife, outer white membrane removed	1
1/4 cup	miso	60 mL
1 1/2	medium tomatoes, cut into large cubes	1 1/2
2 cups	hot filtered or spring water (see Tips, right)	500 mL

Preparation: 10 minutes
Dehydration: 1 hour
Equipment: blender, dehydrator

Makes 4 portions

1. *Vegetables:* In blender, blend all vegetables with tarragon, salt and pepper, then place on a dehydrator tray. Dehydrate at 105°F (41°C) for 1 hour.

2. *Broth:* In blender, combine all ingredients except water and blend into a liquid and evenly consistent paste. Pour into a bowl and add hot water. Stir with a whisk until mixture is evenly consistent.

3. Divide vegetables among soup bowls and pour broth on top.

TIPS

To ensure that the hot water used in this recipe is below 105°F (41°C) and won't destroy any of the enzymes in the ingredients, bring water to a boil and set aside to cool slightly, for 2 to 3 minutes.

These vegetables can be replaced with any other vegetables of your choosing.

Keeps 3 days in the refrigerator in two separate, airtight containers (1 for vegetables and 1 for broth).

Salads

Christmas Kale Salad

2 lbs	kale (about 40 leaves)	1 kg
1½ tsp	sea salt, divided	7 mL
½ tsp	cumin	2 mL
⅛ tsp	ground black pepper	0.5 mL
2½ tbsp	balsamic vinegar	37 mL
¼ cup	olive oil	60 mL
½	medium cauliflower, diced (approx.)	½
1½ cups	julienned red bell pepper	375 mL
¼ cup	thinly sliced red onion	60 mL
2 tbsp	pine nuts	30 mL

Preparation: 15 minutes

Makes 4 portions

1. To trim kale, hold stem in one hand, pull leaf firmly with other hand to separate. Save stems for a juice recipe. Cut kale leaves into thin slivers.

2. Mix kale with ½ tsp (2 mL) of the sea salt to tenderize it. Set aside.

3. Using a whisk, blend together remaining 1 tsp (5 mL) salt, cumin, black pepper, balsamic vinegar and olive oil.

4. In a salad bowl, combine kale, dressing and remaining ingredients.

TIPS

This salad should ideally be prepared 1 to 2 hours ahead of time. This will allow the kale to continue draining and the salad's full flavor to be released.

Keeps 5 days in the refrigerator in an airtight container.

Tabbouleh Flower

1/2	medium cauliflower, shredded in food processor (approx.)	1/2
1 cup	cubed tomatoes	250 mL
3 cups	finely chopped fresh parsley	750 mL
1/3 cup	firmly packed finely chopped red onion	75 mL
5	fresh mint leaves, finely chopped	5
1 1/2 tsp	sea salt	7 mL
1/8 tsp	ground black pepper	0.5 mL
3 tbsp	freshly squeezed lemon juice	45 mL
1 tbsp	olive oil	15 mL
1	clove garlic, chopped, or 1 tsp (5 mL) Garlic Purée (page 25)	1

Preparation: 20 minutes
Equipment: food processor

Makes 4 portions

1. In a salad bowl, combine all ingredients.

TIP

Keeps 5 days in the refrigerator in an airtight container.

WATER

Water is life!

Dehydration probably represents the most widespread and least understood malaise on the planet. So many unpleasant physical symptoms could be resolved if we only remembered to drink a big glass of water.

What water should one choose? First of all, we avoid drinking water directly from the tap because of its high amounts of chlorine, copper, pharmaceutical products and, in some cases, fluoride. We also avoid drinking water in plastic bottles because of the phthalate content (phthalates are a chemical products that ensure malleability and rigidity in plastic). We now know that phthalates reduce fertility and causes testicular atrophy.

A water filter is therefore a necessity, especially when one lives in the city. On the market one can find a number of devices and technologies for filtering water whose costs vary quite a lot. Our advice: avoid reverse osmosis because it is highly polluting; instead choose charcoal or gravity filters.

Ideally, we recommend that everyone who can fill bottles at a spring where the water has been tested. There is nothing more marvelous than taking the time to go to the country on a Sunday and drink from a pure spring. We have introduced quite a few people to this ritual and all of them feel the difference: they drink more and have since returned to the source.

The best water? It comes from fresh organic fruits and vegetables. This living, structured water will nourish your cells. Lettuce, cucumber and celery, in particular, contain 98 percent water. A true fountain of youth!

Waldorf Salad

4	apples, cut into large cubes	4
2 tbsp	freshly squeezed lemon juice	30 mL
8	stalks celery, cut into large cubes	8
1/3 cup	finely chopped green onion	75 mL
1 cup	coarsely chopped walnuts	250 mL
3/4 cup	Cashew Nut Cheese (page 125)	175 mL
2 tbsp	finely chopped fresh parsley	30 mL
1/2 tsp	sea salt	2 mL
1/4 tsp	ground black pepper	1 mL
1	head of lettuce, cut into strips	1

Preparation: 20 minutes

Makes 4 portions

1. Sprinkle some of the lemon juice on the cut apples to prevent them from browning.

2. In a salad bowl, combine all ingredients except lettuce.

3. Lay a bed of lettuce on each dish, then add the salad on top.

TIPS

Keeps 3 days in the refrigerator in an airtight container.

Garnish with lemon wedge, if desired.

COMPOSTING

Compost is food for the earth.

By its fruits, the earth nourishes us in turn. Earth that is not fed, not composted, is gradually drained of its minerals, and so are its fruits. The cycle of nature is relentless. Every conscious gardener knows that it is better to take care of the earth, and that this will keep plants healthy.

Soil depletion, deforestation and the loss of arable land are now a silent catastrophe that have a direct repercussion in our dishes, in which we find fewer and fewer nutrients. Ironically, traditional agriculture attempts to compensate for the weakness of plants by spreading pesticides, herbicides and chemical fertilizers. These products cause even more destruction, weakening the immune system of plants that increasingly fall prey to insects — a chain reaction that leads to the use of even more pesticides.

Compost is therefore precious: it is the key to improving earth that has been depleted. That is why it is our duty to encourage agriculture that is humane, sensitive and organic. By returning food trimmings to the earth, the circle of life makes a complete loop.

By composting, we have also noticed there is a 90 percent reduction in our waste destined for landfill. Thanks to recycling, composting and the purchase of fresh, unpackaged foods, we throw less into the garbage! Get informed about the collection of compost in your city, and if it doesn't exist yet, ask for it.

Fruity Salad

1	large head of lettuce, cut into strips	1
1⅓ cups	arugula	325 mL
1½	zucchini, trimmed, cut into spaghetti	1½
¼	bulb fennel, thinly sliced using a mandoline	¼
1½	oranges, cut into segments	1½
2 cups	clover sprouts	500 mL
	Fig, Apricot and Lime Confit (see below)	
½ cup	Umeboshi Dressing (see right)	125 mL

Preparation: 20 minutes

Equipment: mandoline or spiral cut machine

Makes 4 meal-size portions

1. In a large bowl, combine lettuce and arugula. Place in bottom of 4 individual bowls.

2. Lay cut vegetables and orange segments on top of lettuce mixture. In the center of each bowl, place the clover, topped with a compact ball (¼ of the recipe) of Fig, Apricot and Lime Confit.

3. Sprinkle with dressing just before serving.

Fig, Apricot and Lime Confit

2 tbsp	freshly squeezed lemon juice	30 mL
2 tbsp	freshly squeezed lime juice	30 mL
	Zest of ½ lemon	
	Zest of ½ lime	
2 tsp	sunflower oil	10 mL
1 tbsp	finely chopped gingerroot	15 mL
⅓ cup	dried Calimyrna figs, trimmed and cut into strips	75 mL
⅓ cup	dried apricots, trimmed and cut into strips	75 mL
4 tsp	water	20 mL
⅛ tsp	sea salt	0.5 mL
Pinch	ground black pepper	Pinch

Soaking: 1 night

Preparation: 5 minutes

Makes 1 cup (250 mL)

1. In a bowl, combine all ingredients and mix together by hand.

2. Refrigerate and let marinate at least 1 night.

TIP

Keeps 2 weeks in the refrigerator in an airtight container.

Umeboshi Dressing

2 tbsp	umeboshi paste	30 mL
1/2 cup	kombucha vinegar or 1/3 cup (75 mL) apple cider vinegar	125 mL
1/4 cup	wheat-free tamari sauce or nama shoyu	60 mL
1/2 cup	olive oil	125 mL
1/2 cup	water	125 mL
1 1/2 tsp	sesame oil (see Tips, right)	7 mL

Preparation: 10 minutes

Equipment: blender

Makes about 2 cups (500 mL)

1. In blender, combine all ingredients and blend until thickened into a sauce of even consistency.

TIPS

If you're following a completely raw food diet, look for untoasted sesame oil that is completely unrefined with the label "cold-pressed."

Keeps 1 month in the refrigerator in an airtight container.

Creamy Salad

4	carrots, grated	4
1	medium cabbage, cut into thin strips (about 5 cups/1.25 L)	1
1/4 cup	finely chopped onion	60 mL
1 cup	Mustard-Agave Dressing (see below)	250 mL
1/4 tsp	sea salt	1 mL
1/4 tsp	ground black pepper	1 mL

Preparation: 20 minutes

Makes 4 portions

1. In a salad bowl, combine all ingredients and blend by hand.

TIPS

This salad achieves its full flavor once it has marinated. It is therefore better to prepare it 1 to 2 hours ahead of time.

Keeps 5 to 7 days in the refrigerator in an airtight container.

Mustard-Agave Dressing

1/2 cup	cashew nuts	125 mL
1/2 cup	olive oil	125 mL
1/2 cup	sunflower oil	125 mL
1/3 cup	apple cider vinegar	75 mL
1/4 cup	agave nectar	60 mL
1 1/2 cups	water	375 mL
1 tbsp	Homemade Mustard (page 163) or strong mustard	15 mL
2 tsp	Garlic Purée (page 25) or 1 clove garlic	10 mL
2 tsp	sea salt	10 mL

Soaking: 4 hours
Preparation: 10 minutes
Equipment: blender

Makes about (3 1/2 cups) 875 mL

1. *Soaking:* In a bowl, soak cashew nuts in water for 4 hours. Rinse thoroughly and discard soaking water.

2. In blender, combine all ingredients including soaked drained cashews and blend to a creamy and evenly consistent sauce without pieces of cashew nut.

TIP

Keeps 2 weeks in the refrigerator in an airtight container.

Caesar Salad

1	heart of romaine lettuce, chopped	1
2 tbsp	finely chopped sun-dried tomatoes	30 mL
1 tbsp	capers	15 mL
3 tbsp	Caesar Sauce (see right)	45 mL
¼ cup	Croutons (see right)	60 mL
1 tbsp	Crumesan (page 161)	15 mL

Preparation: 5 minutes

Makes 1 meal-size portion

1. In a salad bowl, combine lettuce, sun-dried tomatoes and capers with Caesar Sauce.

2. Place on a plate, then sprinkle with Croutons and Crumesan. Serve cold.

Caesar Sauce

1 cup	cashew nuts	250 mL
1 cup	water, divided	250 mL
2 tbsp	freshly squeezed lemon juice	30 mL
1/2	clove garlic or 1/2 tsp (2 mL) Garlic Purée (page 25)	1/2
1 tbsp	Homemade Mustard (page 163) or strong mustard	15 mL
1 tsp	sea salt	5 mL
1/2 tsp	ground black pepper	2 mL

Soaking: 4 hours
Preparation: 10 minutes
Equipment: blender

Makes about 1 3/4 cups (425 mL)

1. *Soaking:* In a bowl, soak cashew nuts in water to cover for 4 hours. Rinse thoroughly and discard soaking water.

2. In blender, combine half the water, soaked drained cashews and remaining ingredients and blend to a thick and evenly consistent sauce without pieces of cashew.

3. Add remaining water and blend into a creamy and evenly consistent sauce.

TIP

Keeps 2 weeks in the refrigerator in an airtight container.

Croutons

1 cup	ground flax seeds	250 mL
2 cups	moist nut pulp (see Tips, right)	500 mL
1/2	zucchini, diced (approx.)	1/2
2 tbsp	olive oil	30 mL
1 tbsp	nutritional yeast	15 mL
1 1/4 tsp	sea salt	6 mL
1 tsp	dried basil	5 mL
1 tsp	dried sage	5 mL
1 tsp	dried marjoram	5 mL
1 tsp	ground cumin	5 mL
1 tsp	chili powder	5 mL
1/2 tsp	ground black pepper	2 mL
1/4 tsp	dried oregano	1 mL
1/4 tsp	garlic powder	1 mL

Preparation: 15 minutes
Dehydration: 12 hours
Equipment: dehydrator

Makes about 200 croutons

1. In a bowl, blend all ingredients by hand to obtain an even and consistent paste.

2. On a large cutting board, spread mixture into a pancake of about 1/4-inch (0.5 cm) thickness.

3. Using a knife, cut pancake into small 1/2-inch (1 cm) cubes.

4. Separate cubes and spread them on two dehydrator trays.

5. Set dehydrator temperature to 105°F (41°C). Place trays inside and leave in dehydrator for about 12 hours. Croutons should be thoroughly dry and crunchy.

TIPS

Nut pulp is the pulp remaining in the filter after making a nut milk.

Keeps 2 months in the refrigerator in an airtight container.

Greek Salad with Feta

1	medium cucumber, cut into ³⁄₄-inch (2 cm) cubes (about 2 cups/500 mL)	1
2¹⁄₂	medium tomatoes, cut into ³⁄₄-inch (2 cm) cubes (about 2¹⁄₂ cups/625 mL)	2¹⁄₂
³⁄₄	medium zucchini, cut into ³⁄₄-inch (2 cm) cubes	³⁄₄
2 cups	cubed red bell pepper (about ³⁄₄ inch/2 cm)	500 mL
¹⁄₂ cup	sliced red onion	125 mL
1 cup	watercress	250 mL
2 tbsp	coarsely chopped fresh parsley, firmly packed	30 mL
¹⁄₂ cup	fresh dill, finely chopped, firmly packed	125 mL
¹⁄₄ cup	whole kalamata olives, pitted	60 mL
¹⁄₂ cup	Greek Dressing (see below)	125 mL
4	large handfuls spinach	4
24	pieces Coco-Brazil Feta (see right)	24

Preparation: 15 minutes

Makes 4 portions

1. In a large salad bowl, combine cubed vegetables, red onion, chopped herbs, olives and dressing.

2. Lay a bed of spinach in 4 bowls and place salad on top.

3. Top each salad with 6 cubes of Coco-Brazil Feta.

TIP
Keeps 4 days in the refrigerator in an airtight container.

Greek Dressing

2 tbsp	lemon juice	30 mL
³⁄₄ tsp	Garlic Purée (page 25) or ³⁄₄ clove garlic, minced	3 mL
¹⁄₂ cup	sunflower oil	125 mL
¹⁄₂ cup	apple cider vinegar	125 mL
¹⁄₂ cup	olive oil	125 mL
1 tbsp	chopped fresh tarragon	15 mL
1 tsp	agave nectar	5 mL
1 tsp	sea salt	5 mL
¹⁄₂ tsp	dried basil	2 mL
¹⁄₂ tsp	dried parsley	2 mL
¹⁄₄ tsp	dried oregano	2 mL
¹⁄₄ tsp	dried thyme	2 mL
¹⁄₈ tsp	ground cayenne pepper	0.5 mL

Preparation: 10 minutes

Makes about 1¹⁄₂ cups (375 mL)

1. In blender or using a whisk, combine all ingredients and blend into a liquid and evenly consistent dressing.

TIPS
This dressing tends to separate in the refrigerator; always blend it thoroughly before using it.

Keeps 2 weeks in the refrigerator in an airtight container.

Coco-Brazil Feta

1/2 cup	Brazil nuts	125 mL
4 tsp	freshly squeezed lemon juice	20 mL
1 cup	coconut butter, softened	250 mL
1/4 cup	water	60 mL
1 tbsp	olive oil	15 mL
4 tsp	apple cider vinegar	20 mL
4 tsp	nutritional yeast	20 mL
1 tsp	sea salt	5 mL
1 tsp	dried basil	5 mL
1 tsp	dried parsley	5 mL
1/2 tsp	dried oregano	2 mL
1/2 tsp	dried thyme	2 mL
1/8 tsp	ground cayenne pepper	0.5 mL

Preparation: 15 minutes
Equipment: food processor or blender

Makes 120 feta cubes

1. In food processor, reduce Brazil nuts to a butter that is as liquid and creamy as possible.

2. Add remaining ingredients to food processor and blend to obtain an evenly consistent paste.

3. Spread this mixture in a 1/2-inch (1 cm) thick layer in one or several deep dishes.

4. Refrigerate for 3 hours.

5. Cut slab into 3/4-inch (2 cm) cubes before removing feta from dishes.

TIP

Keeps 2 weeks in the refrigerator in an airtight container.

Madras Salad

Creamy Indian Sauce

1/4 cup	tahini (sesame paste) or cashew nut butter, raw, if possible	60 mL
2 tbsp	sunflower oil	30 mL
2 tbsp	water	30 mL
2 tbsp	apple cider vinegar	30 mL
1 tbsp	sea salt	15 mL
2 tsp	curry powder	10 mL
1 1/2 tsp	ground coriander seeds	7 mL
1 tsp	turmeric	5 mL
1 tsp	ground cumin	5 mL
1/2 tsp	ground ginger	2 mL
1/2 tsp	ground black pepper	2 mL
6	medium carrots, shredded	6
1/2	medium cauliflower, cut into small cubes	1/2
1/4	medium onion, finely chopped	1/4
1/2 cup	finely chopped fresh cilantro, firmly packed	125 mL
1/4 cup	currants	60 mL
2 tbsp	black sesame seeds	30 mL

Preparation: 15 minutes
Equipment: blender

Makes 4 portions

1. *Creamy Indian Sauce:* In blender, combine all ingredients and blend into a smooth sauce.

2. Place vegetables, Creamy Indian sauce and remaining ingredients in a bowl and mix together by hand so that vegetables are thoroughly coated in spices.

TIP

Keeps 4 to 5 days in the refrigerator in an airtight container.

Polynesian Salad

8	large handfuls arugula or baby spinach	8
1/2 cup	Asian Dressing (see below)	125 mL
	Flesh of 2 young coconuts (Thai coconuts)	
4	pears or 1 Asian pear, cut into strips (approx.)	4
2	kiwis, cut into slices	2
2 cups	julienned snow pea pods	500 mL
2 tbsp	lime juice	30 mL
1/2 cup	coarsely chopped cilantro leaves	125 mL
2 to 4 tsp	hot pepper flakes	10 to 20 mL
1/2 tsp	sea salt	2 mL
1/2 tsp	finely chopped gingerroot	2 mL

Preparation: 10 minutes

Makes 4 portions

1. In a bowl, combine arugula and Asian dressing. Lay a bed of arugula equally in 4 bowls.

2. In a salad bowl, blend remaining ingredients. Place a mound of mixture in the center of each bed of arugula.

TIP

Keeps 2 to 3 days in the refrigerator in an airtight container.

Asian Dressing

1 cup	sunflower oil	250 mL
2 tbsp	nama shoyu	30 mL
2 tbsp	freshly squeezed lemon juice	30 mL
1 tbsp	Ginger Juice (page 24) or chopped gingerroot	15 mL
1 tbsp	Garlic Purée (page 25) or 3 cloves garlic, chopped	15 mL
1/2 cup	water	125 mL
1 tsp	agave nectar	5 mL
1 tsp	ground coriander seeds	5 mL
1/2 tsp	sesame oil (see Tips, page 89)	2 mL
1/8 tsp	sea salt	0.5 mL
1/2 cup	firmly packed coarsely chopped fresh cilantro (leaves and stems)	125 mL

Preparation: 10 minutes
Equipment: blender

Makes about 1 1/2 cups (375 mL)

1. In blender, combine all ingredients except cilantro and blend to a dressing of even consistency.

2. Add fresh cilantro and pulse briefly to leave small pieces of leaves intact.

TIP

Keeps 2 weeks in the refrigerator in an airtight container.

Rémoulade Salad

1/3 cup	Caper Aïoli (page 166)	75 mL
2 tbsp	sunflower oil	30 mL
2 tbsp	capers, coarsely chopped	30 mL
1 tbsp	freshly squeezed lemon juice	15 mL
1 tsp	Homemade Mustard (page 163) or strong mustard	5 mL
1/2 tsp	sea salt	2 mL
1/4 tsp	ground black pepper	1 mL
5 cups	shredded celeriac	1.25 L

Preparation: 10 minutes

Makes 4 portions

1. Using a whisk, combine all ingredients except celeriac and blend into an evenly consistent sauce.

2. Place celeriac in a salad bowl. Add sauce and mix together.

TIP

Keeps 5 to 7 days in the refrigerator in an airtight container.

Cucumber Dill Salad

	Zest of 2 lemons	
1/4 cup	firmly packed coarsely chopped dill (leaves and stems)	60 mL
3 tbsp	finely chopped red onion	45 mL
2 tbsp	olive oil	30 mL
1 tbsp	freshly squeezed lemon juice	15 mL
2 tsp	balsamic vinegar	10 mL
1 tsp	sea salt	5 mL
1/2 tsp	ground black pepper	2 mL
2	medium cucumbers, cut in half lengthwise, then sliced diagonally	2

Preparation: 5 minutes

Makes 4 portions

1. In a salad bowl, using a whisk, combine all ingredients except cucumbers to make an evenly consistent dressing.

2. Add cucumbers and combine with dressing.

TIPS

This salad will become more flavorful if it stands for at least 20 minutes before being served.

Keeps 3 days in the refrigerator in an airtight container.

Bloody Caesar Salad

3	heads romaine lettuce, cut into pieces	3
1	large beet, shredded	1
$1/2$	red onion, finely chopped	$1/2$
$1/2$	red bell pepper, cut into cubes	$1/2$
$3/4$ cup	goji berries	175 mL
$1^1/_2$ tsp	celery seeds	7 mL
$3/4$ cup	Greek Dressing (page 94)	175 mL
30	pieces Coco-Brazil Feta (page 95)	30
$1/2$ cup	finely chopped sun-dried tomatoes	125 mL
$1/2$ cup	shelled hemp seeds	125 mL

Preparation: 15 minutes

Makes 4 portions

1. In a salad bowl, combine lettuce, beet, red onion, bell pepper, goji berries and celery seeds with Greek Dressing.

2. Divide salad into 4 bowls and garnish with Coco-Brazil Feta, pieces of sun-dried tomato and hemp seeds. Serve cold.

ACID-BASE BALANCE

The human body is an ecosystem in itself.

Our bodies, just like the planet, have their rivers, seasons, acid rains and greenhouse gases. As an integral part of nature, our bodies therefore function under the same laws. We consider that every gesture, every movement, every drop of water affects the ecosystem on the macrocosmic level, the planet, as much as on the microcosmic level, the cell.

Like the ocean, the body has specific barometers for temperature, salt and mineral levels. Some of us remember the physics courses in which we first learned to observe the pH (potential hydrogen) level of a solution. For others, pH makes us think of the weekly check of the swimming pool or whirlpool bath. Every chemical element has a precise pH value that is acid or alkaline. Humans, just like plants and animals, have an alkaline pH level of about 7.38.

To maintain this state, in which homeostasis is at its peak, the body needs minerals, oxygen and movement. Stagnation in lymph or interstitial fluids, a lack of minerals in the diet or a period of stress will affect the body's acid-base balance. Adrenalin, cortisol and muscle tension thus become acidifying agents related to stress that can damage health much more quickly than a burger and a carbonated beverage.

Deep breathing, cardio-respiratory coherence and aerobic physical activity can alkalinize even more than a glass of wheatgrass juice. But what happens if we give ourselves every chance — by having a relaxed way of life, an open attitude, daily physical activity and foods high in minerals and oxygen? That's what we call being fully alive!

Orange Jumble Salad

2	medium bulbs fennel, thinly sliced	2
1/3	red bell pepper, cut into thin strips	1/3
4	orange segments	4
	Flesh of 2 avocados, cut into cubes	
1 cup	coarsely chopped fresh cilantro	250 mL
2 tbsp	olive oil	30 mL
1 tbsp	ground coriander seeds	15 mL
1/2 tsp	sea salt	2 mL
1/2 tsp	lemon juice	2 mL
1/4 tsp	orange essence or orange zest	1 mL

Optional

1 tbsp	firmly packed arame	15 mL

Preparation: 15 minutes

Makes 4 portions

1. Blend all ingredients in a salad bowl.

2. If using arame, soak in water for 5 minutes. Use as a garnish, if desired. Serve cold.

SUGARS

Chlorophyll is the primary producer of sugar.

Starting with energy from the Sun, it weaves carbon and water into glucose molecules. What an incredible and fundamental process of life!

It is thanks to these carbohydrates that nature builds itself. The cellulose that makes up a tree is, in fact, just a long chain of glucose, also called polysaccharides. An apple or a sweet potato thus represent reserves of solar energy transformed by chlorophyll and stored in the plant to survive winter or to attract a hungry animal that will spread the seeds.

The simple sugar found in an apple does not last long in nature and will quickly be consumed by an animal or bacteria. It is the same in the human body. Once it is in the blood, glucose must quickly be transformed by the liver into glycogen, the principal food for the cells. The surplus of glucose will be transformed into stored fat. These fats, being materials that are easier to store and less dangerous for the organism, will turn into glycogen, then fuel if needed. In this way, it is understandable that catastrophic weight gain in North America is not caused by fat, but by sugar. Pasteurized fruit juices, carbonated beverages, bread and pasta are processed and refined sugars and are, as such, a cause of weight gain because they are consumed in too large quantities.

On the other hand, natural and raw sugars are essential to our diet. We find them in fruits and vegetables, where they are supplemented by vitamins and fiber. They are digested slowly and provide energy in a healthy way.

And so, an apple is perfect if it is eaten as is; it contains an enormous amount of nutrients. On the other hand, processed into pasteurized juice, it will be digested very quickly. The precious fiber, which serves to trap and distribute fructose slowly, is absent, so pasteurized juice increases glycemia much more quickly and unbalances homeostasis.

Lumen Salad

¼ cup	firmly packed dried arame (makes ¾ cup/ 175 mL moistened)	60 mL
¼ cup	firmly packed dried wakame, cut into large cubes with scissors (makes ½ cup/125 mL moistened)	60 mL
3	medium carrots, peeled and cut into thin strips with a vegetable peeler	3
1 cup	broccoli florets	250 mL
⅓	leek, finely chopped	⅓
1½ tbsp	nama shoyu	22 mL
1 tbsp	freshly squeezed lemon juice	15 mL
1 tsp	sesame oil (see Tips, right)	5 mL
2 tsp	black sesame seeds	10 mL
2 tsp	white sesame seeds	10 mL
½ tsp	agave nectar	2 mL
⅛ tsp	ground black pepper	0.5 mL
⅛ tsp	ground cayenne pepper	0.5 mL

Soaking: 10 to 15 minutes
Preparation: 15 minutes
Equipment: vegetable peeler

Makes 4 portions

1. *Soaking:* In a bowl, soak arame and wakame seaweed in 1 cup (250 mL) water while preparing the rest of the ingredients, 10 to 15 minutes. The water for soaking will not be used in this recipe, but can be saved to make a soup.

2. Drain seaweed and place in a salad bowl. Add remaining ingredients and mix together.

TIPS

If you're following a completely raw food diet, look for untoasted sesame oil that is completely unrefined with the label "cold-pressed."

Keeps 4 days in the refrigerator in an airtight container.

Aztec Salad

1/3 cup	quinoa	75 mL
4	stalks celery, sliced diagonally	4
1	medium red bell pepper, cut into cubes	1
1 cup	corn kernels (about 2 cobs)	250 mL
1 cup	wax beans, cut into diagonal pieces	250 mL
1/4 cup	firmly packed finely chopped fresh cilantro	60 mL
1/4 cup	finely chopped green onion	60 mL
3 tbsp	Chipotle Sauce (see below)	45 mL

Soaking: 8 to 12 hours
Germination: 12 hours
Preparation: 10 minutes

Makes 4 portions

1. *Soaking:* Two days before ready to make the salad, sprout quinoa. Soak overnight in water for 8 to 12 hours. Rinse, then let sprout in open air for 12 hours, rinsing 2 to 3 times during the day (see germination technique on page 19).

2. The same day you are ready to make salad, blend all ingredients in a salad bowl.

TIP

Keeps 3 to 4 days in the refrigerator in an airtight container.

Chipotle Sauce

2	medium dried chipotle peppers	2
1/2 cup	water or soaking water from chipotle peppers	125 mL
6	seedless dates or 1/4 cup (60 mL) Date Paste (page 25)	6
1/2 cup	sunflower oil	125 mL
5 tbsp	apple cider vinegar	75 mL
2 tsp	freshly squeezed lemon juice	10 mL
1	clove garlic or 1 tsp (5 mL) Garlic Purée (page 25)	1
2 tbsp	firmly packed chopped fresh cilantro	30 mL
1/2 tsp	sea salt	2 mL
1/2 cup	sunflower seeds, ground	125 mL

Soaking: 30 minutes to overnight
Preparation: 10 minutes
Equipment: blender

Makes about 2 cups (500 mL)

1. *Soaking:* In a bowl, cover chipotle peppers with water and let soak for at least 30 minutes or up to overnight to soften them. For a hotter dressing, use the soaking water in this recipe. It is also possible to remove the seeds from the peppers to make them less hot without altering the taste.

2. In blender, combine all ingredients except ground sunflower seeds and blend into an evenly consistent liquid.

3. Add ground sunflower seeds and continue blending until sauce is smooth and creamy.

TIP

Keeps 2 weeks in the refrigerator in an airtight container.

Crudessence Salad

1	beet, reduced to spaghetti using spiral cut machine (optional)	1
1	large head lettuce, cut into pieces	1
12	Beet Crackers or Sun-dried Tomato Crackers (pages 149 and 150)	12
½ cup	Sauerkraut (page 131)	125 mL
1 cup	Buddha Nuts (page 153)	250 mL
½ cup	Hummus Sun Spread (page 114)	125 mL
1	medium carrot, shredded (about ½ cup/125 mL)	1
1	avocado, thinly sliced	1
1	tomato, cut into 8 segments	1
1⅓ cups	clover sprouts	325 mL
¾ cup	dressing of your choice	175 mL

Soaking: a few minutes
Preparation: 10 minutes
Equipment: blender, spiral cut machine

Makes 4 portions

1. In a large container of cold water, soak beet spaghetti. Set aside.

2. On a bed of lettuce, place remaining ingredients except beets, clover shoots and dressing without blending them, then top with clover shoots. Serve dressing in a separate container.

3. Rinse beets thoroughly until they no longer color the water. Drain before using them to garnish the dish.

THE 5 FLAVORS

Sweet, salty, bitter, sour and umami.

This is the range of primary flavors, which form the basis of our cuisine. Just like an artist, who combines primary colors to create an infinite palette of other colors, the chefs from our restaurant Crudessence use primary flavors to create an infinite number of additional flavors. All you need is to apply these five flavors on the culinary canvas with a little inspiration to achieve works of art. Culinary expression thus becomes highly creative.

You'll find that it is easier to work with five flavors than 100,000 ingredients. What's more, it's pointless to think about classifying them... just use your tongue! In fact, you'll discover that certain ingredients possess several balanced flavors that harmonize in a particular way.

For example, the popular Middle Eastern hummus contains the five flavors on a canvas of chickpeas: (tahini = sour, lemon = bitter, garlic and paprika = umami, salt = salty, cooked chickpeas = sweet). Whether it is guacamole from Mexico on a canvas of avocado or a classic Italian dressing on a canvas of olive oil, the principle of the flavors cannot be ignored.

And so, you can replace one of the ingredients used in our recipes with another ingredient covering the same flavor. In this way, our recipes will become yours.

Spreads

Hummus Sun Spread

2/3 cup	unpeeled almonds	150 mL
2 cups	coarsely chopped peeled zucchini	500 mL
3/4 cup	tahini (sesame paste), raw, if possible	175 mL
1	clove garlic or 1 tsp (5 mL) Garlic Purée (page 25)	1
6 tbsp	freshly squeezed lemon juice	90 mL
2 tbsp	olive oil	30 mL
2 tsp	cumin	10 mL
1 1/2 tsp	sea salt	7 mL
1/4 tsp	ground black pepper	1 mL

Soaking: 8 hours
Preparation: 15 minutes
Equipment: blender

Makes 4 portions or about 3 cups (750 mL)

1. *Soaking:* In a bowl, soak unpeeled almonds in water to cover for 8 hours. Rinse thoroughly and discard soaking water.

2. In blender, combine all ingredients including soaked almonds and reduce to a smooth, creamy paste.

TIPS

Serve as a dip with raw vegetables, in a salad, on crackers or as a sandwich, either wrapped in lettuce or spread on raw bread.

Keeps 3 to 4 days in the refrigerator in an airtight container.

Pecan Dill Terrine

1 cup	sunflower seeds	250 mL
2/3 cup	pecans	150 mL
1/4 cup	sunflower oil	60 mL
2 tbsp	apple cider vinegar	30 mL
2 tbsp	freshly squeezed lemon juice	30 mL
2 tbsp	water	30 mL
1/2 cup	firmly packed coarsely chopped fresh parsley (leaves and stems)	125 mL
1/4 cup	firmly packed coarsely chopped fresh dill (leaves and stems)	60 mL
1	medium clove garlic or 1 tsp (5 mL) Garlic Purée (page 25)	1
1 tsp	sea salt	5 mL

Soaking: 8 hours
Preparation: 20 minutes
Equipment: food processor

Makes 4 portions or about 2 1/3 cups (575 mL)

1. *Soaking:* In a bowl, soak sunflower seeds and pecans in water to cover for 8 hours. Rinse thoroughly and discard soaking water.

2. In food processor, reduce sunflower seeds and pecans to a purée.

3. Add remaining ingredients and blend until mixture is smooth and creamy.

TIPS

Serve as a dip with raw vegetables, in a salad, on crackers or as a sandwich, either wrapped in lettuce or spread on raw bread.

Keeps 3 to 4 days in the refrigerator in an airtight container.

Kalamata Olive Tapenade

²/₃ cup	sunflower seeds	150 mL
1 cup	firmly packed pitted kalamata olives	250 mL
1¹/₂	medium clove garlic or 1¹/₂ tsp (7 mL) Garlic Purée (page 25)	1¹/₂
¹/₃ cup	coarsely chopped red onion	75 mL
2 tbsp	sunflower oil	30 mL
2 tbsp	balsamic vinegar	30 mL
2 tbsp	freshly squeezed lemon juice	30 mL
¹/₄ cup	ground sunflower seeds	60 mL
2 tbsp	chopped fresh oregano	30 mL
¹/₄ cup	firmly packed chopped fresh parsley (leaves and stems)	60 mL

Soaking: 8 hours
Preparation: 15 minutes
Equipment: food processor

Makes 4 portions or about 2 cups (500 mL)

1. *Soaking:* In a bowl, soak sunflower seeds in water to cover for 8 hours. Rinse thoroughly and discard soaking water.

2. In food processor, blend all ingredients except ground sunflower seeds, oregano and chopped parsley to a smooth, creamy paste.

3. Add ground sunflower seeds and blend again for 1 minute to obtain an evenly consistent mixture.

4. Spoon mixture into serving bowl, then stir in oregano and parsley.

TIPS

Serve as a dip with raw vegetables, in a salad, on crackers or as a sandwich, either wrapped in lettuce or spread on raw bread.

Keeps 3 to 4 days in the refrigerator in an airtight container.

Macadamia Ricotta Cheese

1⅓ cups	macadamia nuts	325 mL
⅓ cup	water	75 mL
2 tbsp	freshly squeezed lemon juice	30 mL
¼	clove garlic or ¼ tsp (1 mL) Garlic Purée (page 25)	¼
½ tsp	sea salt	2 mL
⅛ tsp	ground black pepper	0.5 mL

Preparation: 10 minutes
Equipment: food processor

Makes about 1⅔ cups (400 mL)

1. In food processor, reduce macadamia nuts to small pieces.
2. Add remaining ingredients and blend for a few seconds to form an emulsion. The cheese will turn white and creamy with small crunchy pieces of nut.

TIPS

Serve as a dip with raw vegetables, in a salad, on crackers or as a sandwich, either wrapped in lettuce or spread on raw bread.

Keeps 2 weeks in the refrigerator in an airtight container.

PROTEINS

As some of you have already experienced, vegetarians face questions from the people around them about protein: "Are you sure you're getting enough proteins?" This question comes up even more often when you follow a living food diet!

In perspective, mother's milk, a unique fuel that helps a newborn grow in a healthy way and double its weight in a few months, contains just 6 percent proteins. A gorilla, a muscular mammal that does not appear to lack protein, consumes a diet consisting of 50 percent green leaves, 35 percent fresh fruits and 15 percent roots, tubers, beans and a tiny amount of mosquitoes. In short, it is a raw food eater and mostly vegan.

The fear of a lack of protein is most pronounced in our society. In fact, protein is simply a large chain of amino acids. In order to assimilate protein, the body must break down the chain with the help of digestive enzymes and gastric acids. It is a laborious process that requires a great deal of energy. After breaking down into microscopic building materials, the amino acids are absorbed into the intestines and then reconstructed into human proteins and used in many functions, including the formation of muscle fibers, enzymes, hormones and cells.

Finally, the plant world contains an ample amount of protein to support the needs of an athlete or a breast-feeding mother. The trick is simple: variety! Green leafy vegetables such as kale and spinach, as well as sunflower seeds and sprouted lentils, are champions in amino acids. Furthermore, spirulina, bee pollen, hemp seeds, buckwheat, pumpkin seeds and chlorella are complete sources of protein.

Oaxaca Spread

2 cups	sunflower seeds	500 mL
1	very small chipotle pepper	1
½ cup	sun-dried tomatoes	125 mL
¾ cup	water	175 mL
1 tbsp	chopped jalapeño pepper, seeds removed	15 mL
¼	clove garlic or ¼ tsp (1 mL) Garlic Purée (page 25)	¼
¼ cup	coarsely chopped fresh cilantro (leaves and stems), firmly packed	60 mL
1 tsp	freshly squeezed lemon juice	5 mL
1 tsp	chili powder	5 mL
¼ tsp	sea salt	1 mL

Soaking: 8 to 12 hours
Preparation: 15 minutes
Equipment: food processor

Makes 4 portions or about 3 cups (750 mL)

1. *Soaking:* In a bowl, soak sunflower seeds in water to cover for 8 hours. Rinse thoroughly and save soaking water. Yields 3 cups (750 mL) of seeds.

2. Cover chipotle pepper with water and let soak for at least 15 minutes or for up to 12 hours. Discard soaking water.

3. Soak sun-dried tomatoes in ¾ cup (175 mL) water for at least 15 minutes or for up to 12 hours. Save soaking water.

4. In food processor, combine all ingredients including soaking water from sunflower seeds and sun-dried tomatoes and blend into a paste of even consistency.

TIPS

Serve as a dip with raw vegetables, in a salad, on crackers or as a sandwich, either wrapped in lettuce or spread on raw bread.

Keeps 3 to 4 days in the refrigerator in an airtight container.

"Ocean" Spread

Spread

1 cup	sunflower seeds	250 mL
1/3 cup	walnuts	75 mL
1/4 cup	dulse seaweed, cut into very small pieces using scissors	60 mL
1 tbsp	wheat-free tamari sauce	15 mL

Vegetable mixture

2 to 3	stalks celery, diced	2 to 3
2 tbsp	finely chopped green onion, shallot or red onion	30 mL
2 tbsp	finely chopped fresh dill	30 mL
	"Mayonnaise" (see below)	

Soaking: 8 hours
Preparation: 20 minutes
Equipment: food processor

Makes 4 portions or about 2 cups (500 mL)

1. *Soaking:* In a bowl, soak sunflower seeds and walnuts to cover in water for 8 hours. Rinse seeds and nuts thoroughly and discard soaking water.

2. *Spread:* In food processor, combine all ingredients and blend into an evenly consistent paste.

3. In a salad bowl, blend spread, cut vegetable mixture and "Mayonnaise."

TIPS

Serve as a dip with raw vegetables, in a salad, on crackers or as a sandwich, either wrapped in lettuce or spread on raw bread.

Keeps 5 days in the refrigerator in an airtight container.

"Mayonnaise"

1/2 cup	cashew nuts	125 mL
1 1/2	cloves garlic or 1 1/2 tsp (7 mL) Garlic Purée (page 25)	1 1/2
2 tbsp	freshly squeezed lemon juice	30 mL
1 tbsp	Homemade Mustard (page 163) or strong mustard	15 mL
1/2 cup	macadamia nuts	125 mL
1/4 cup	water	60 mL
3/4 tsp	sea salt	3 mL

Soaking: 4 hours
Equipment: blender

Makes 1 cup (250 mL)

1. *Soaking:* In a bowl, soak cashew nuts in water to cover for 4 hours. Rinse thoroughly and discard soaking water.

2. In blender, combine all ingredients including soaked cashews and blend to a creamy sauce without pieces of nut. Add more water, if necessary.

TIP

Keeps 3 to 4 days in the refrigerator in an airtight container.

Country Spread

1 cup	sunflower seeds	250 mL
2/3 cup	walnuts	150 mL
1 cup	firmly packed mushroom stems (or whole mushrooms, cut into pieces)	250 mL
1/4 cup	coarsely chopped fresh dill (leaves and stems)	60 mL
2 tbsp	nama shoyu or wheat-free tamari sauce	30 mL
1	clove garlic or 1 tsp (5 mL) Garlic Purée (page 25)	1
1/2 tsp	ground black pepper	2 mL
1/4 tsp	sea salt	1 mL

Soaking: 8 hours

Preparation: 15 minutes

Equipment: food processor

Makes 4 portions or 2½ cups (625 mL)

1. *Soaking:* In a bowl, soak sunflower seeds and walnuts in water to cover for 8 hours. Rinse seeds and nuts thoroughly and discard soaking water.

2. In food processor, reduce walnuts to a purée. Add a little water, if necessary.

3. Add remaining ingredients and blend into a smooth, creamy mixture.

TIPS

This spread is used to stuff Mushroom Caps (page 47). It can also be served as a dip with raw vegetables, in a salad, on crackers or as a sandwich, either wrapped in lettuce or spread on raw bread.

Keeps 4 days in the refrigerator in an airtight container.

GARDENS IN THE CITY

Being idealistic and slightly revolutionary, we have always dreamed of a verdant city with trees everywhere and roofs covered in plants. Not decorative plants and trees, but nutritious, functional plants and fruit trees. Food and medicine growing in the city!

As a result of food scarcity due to the American embargo, the inhabitants of Cuba have proven to us that, through communal effort, this dream can quickly become a reality. They have achieved the near impossible by using every little plot of earth to cultivate vegetables, plant trees and keep a few chickens. In this way, they have once again become self-sufficient in terms of food security.

Thanks to private backyards, community gardens, edible rooftop gardening and many university projects, this dream is taking shape in Montreal. Even the Palais des Congrès convention center in the heart of the city provides us with hundreds of square feet (or square meters) to grow our own vegetables and herbs. In Quebec, a garden project by Crudessence in association with Alternative is the first rooftop gardening project to produce food for restaurants. An experiment worth cultivating! Furthermore, not only will the plants feed city dwellers, they will also help to refresh the city, eliminate heat islands, reduce greenhouse gases and allow the re-establishment of bees.

Pistachio Basil Pesto

¹/₂ cup	pistachio nuts	125 mL
¹/₃ cup	cashew nuts	75 mL
1 cup	firmly packed chopped fresh basil (leaves and stems)	125 mL
1¹/₂	cloves garlic or 1¹/₂ tsp (7 mL) Garlic Purée (page 25)	
¹/₂ cup	olive oil	125 mL
¹/₂ tsp	sea salt	2 mL

Soaking: 4 hours
Preparation: 15 minutes
Equipment: blender

Makes about 1¹/₂ cups (375 mL)

1. *Soaking:* In a bowl, soak pistachio and cashew nuts in water to cover for 4 hours. Rinse thoroughly after soaking and discard soaking water.

2. In blender, combine all ingredients and reduce to a smooth, creamy paste.

TIP

Keeps 1 week in the refrigerator in an airtight container or 6 months in the freezer.

Fermentation

Cashew Nut Cheese

2 cups	cashew nuts	500 mL
³/₄ cup	water	175 mL
1¹/₂ tbsp	miso or 2 tbsp (30 mL) cashew cheese, already fermented	22 mL
1¹/₂ tsp	coconut oil, melted	7 mL
1 tbsp	freshly squeezed lemon juice	15 mL
¹/₄ tsp	sea salt	1 mL

Soaking: 4 hours

Preparation: 20 minutes

Fermentation: 12 hours

Equipment: blender

Makes about 2 cups (500 mL)

1. *Soaking:* In a bowl, soak cashew nuts in water to cover for 4 hours. Rinse thoroughly and discard soaking water.

2. In blender, combine cashew nuts, ³/₄ cup (175 mL) water and miso (or already fermented cheese) and blend to a creamy consistency until all pieces of cashew nut have disappeared.

3. Place in a salad bowl and cover with plastic wrap resting on cheese. This fermentation is anaerobic.

4. Let ferment for 12 hours at room temperature.

5. Once mixture is fermented, use a spatula to incorporate melted coconut oil, lemon juice and sea salt.

TIPS

This cheese can be served as is, garnished with fresh herbs, or can be used to make "Cheese" Cake (page 198).

Keeps 10 days in the refrigerator in an airtight container.

ENZYMES

These small living things are very popular in the raw food world, but are sometimes misunderstood. Enzymes are functional proteins that exist in nature in thousands of different forms. Enzymes are effective catalyzers of biochemical reactions. They accelerate the digestion of foods and play an active role in building body tissues. There are metabolic enzymes and digestive enzymes.

A number of raw foodists claim that uncooked food retains all its enzymes and that these enzymes will digest the food in the stomach. This is partially true. Heat destroys enzymatic life, and so cooking a food prevents us from fully benefiting from its effects. On the other hand, after digestion, the enzyme will be destroyed because of the stomach's highly acidic pH (pH of 3) and transformed into amino acids. "Pointless to eat raw," you may say!

However, the research done by Dr. Gabriel Cousens confirms that the enzymes in a food will be useful to digesting that food during the first hour of digestion, during which the pH of the stomach is viable (pH of 5). Furthermore, the digested enzymes, transformed into amino acids, are of much higher quality than enzymes that have been destroyed by cooking.

In the Crudessence kitchen, enzymes are the fire of life, helping us to transform foods before they are ingested. Soaking, germination and fermentation are the art of using the power of enzymes outside our bodies. These "micro chefs" do a lot of the work to help us digest food more easily.

Kefir

1/3 cup	agave nectar or Sucanat or organic fair-trade cane sugar	75 mL
7 cups	water	1.75 L
1/4 cup	kefir grains (see Tips, right)	60 mL
1	lemon, sliced	1
4	dried figs or any other dried fruit	4

Preparation: 20 minutes

Fermentation: 2 days

Equipment: 8-cup (2 L) glass container, fine-mesh fabric such as nylon mosquito netting

Makes 8 cups (2 L)

1. In glass container, dissolve sugar in water.

2. Add kefir grains, lemon slices and dried figs. (Do not fill the jar all the way up because carbon dioxide production will result in an increase in volume.)

3. Cover with fine-mesh fabric and attach it with an elastic band or cord (the fabric will allow air to pass through, but not dust). Store in a temperate place (64°F to 75°F/18°C to 24°C), away from light. Let ferment for 2 days. Kefir is ready when figs rise to the surface. During fermentation, the kefir grains proliferate, forming a white, natural deposit.

4. Pour kefir through a sieve to collect seeds. Rinse seeds under running water. They can immediately be placed in a new kefir or kept in water in the refrigerator.

5. Discard dried fruits and squeeze lemon slices into beverage.

6. Kefir is ready to be consumed or bottled and placed in refrigerator to halt fermentation.

TIPS

Fermented for 1 day, kefir will be slightly laxative; fermented 2 to 3 days, it will be full of probiotics.

Keeps 4 days in the refrigerator in an airtight container.

To obtain kefir grains, visit the website www.crudessence.com.

Sauerkraut

1½	medium green cabbage, shredded	1½
1½ tbsp	sea salt (approx.)	22 mL
2 tbsp	juniper berries	30 mL
2	bay leaves	2

Preparation: 30 minutes
Fermentation: 21 days

Makes two 2-cup (500 mL) glass jars or Mason jars

1. In a large salad bowl, combine all ingredients together by hand for a few minutes.

2. Pack mixture tightly in several glass or Mason jars that have already been sterilized. Use hands to press down cabbage. It must be covered in its own water to eliminate all the air from the container. The container must also be filled to the top. Sauerkraut is a fermentation that is anaerobic (without oxygen); the cabbage must be completely immersed. If some pieces rise to the surface, they risk turning moldy. If this happens, they can simply be discarded. The rest of the sauerkraut will not be affected.

3. Place lid on top without sealing jar airtight and cover with a weight.

4. Place jars of sauerkraut in a larger container or a deep dish in order to collect the liquid that may run out during fermentation. Keep away from direct light, in an area where there will be at least a little air circulation.

5. Let ferment 21 days, in a room where the temperature is between 64°F and 75°F (between 18°C and 24°C); fermentation will occur faster or slower depending on the storage temperature.

6. After 21 days, taste sauerkraut. If still too salty, let ferment an additional 72 hours. When sauerkraut is ready, place in refrigerator to slow down fermentation.

TIPS

Whatever quantity one makes, the secret of sauerkraut is to respect the following proportion: the weight of the salt must be equal to 2 percent of the weight of the cabbage. You can also replace one-third of the green cabbage with red cabbage to make red sauerkraut. The spices can be modified and you can add other vegetables.

Keeps 6 months in the refrigerator in an airtight container.

Kimchi

¼ cup	sea salt	60 mL
4 cups	warm water	1 L
1	large napa cabbage, shredded	1
1	medium daikon (Japanese giant white radish), julienned	1
½ tsp	cayenne pepper	2 mL
5	green onions, cut into diagonal pieces	5
2 tsp	Garlic Purée (page 25) or 2 cloves garlic, finely chopped	10 mL
¼ cup	grated gingerroot	60 mL
1 to 3 tbsp	hot pepper flakes	15 to 45 mL
2 tbsp	agave nectar	30 mL
1 tsp	sesame oil (see Tips, right)	5 mL

Preparation: 20 minutes
Fermentation: 3 to 4 days

Makes two 2-cup (500 mL) jars

1. In a salad bowl, dissolve salt in warm water. Add cabbage and daikon. Let stand for 3 to 4 hours.

2. Drain, then rinse cabbage and daikon under running water to remove excess salt.

3. Place in a bowl, add remaining ingredients and blend thoroughly.

4. Pour mixture into a large jar that has already been sterilized. Use hands to press down mixture. It must be covered in its own water to eliminate all the air from the container. The jar must be filled to the top; add water if necessary.

5. Place lid on top without sealing it airtight and cover with a weight.

6. Place jars of kimchi in a larger container or deep dish to collect the liquid that may run out during fermentation. Keep out of direct light, in an area where there is at least a little air circulation. Let marinate at least 3 to 4 days before tasting, but not more than 7 days. Store in refrigerator to slow down fermentation.

TIPS

If you're following a completely raw food diet, look for untoasted sesame oil that is completely unrefined with the label "cold-pressed."

Keeps 6 months in the refrigerator in an airtight glass container.

Nut Yogurt

3/4 cup	cashew nuts	175 mL
1 1/4 cups	water	300 mL
3 tbsp	agave nectar	45 mL
1	packet yogurt base or 1/4 cup (60 mL) yogurt, already fermented or active probiotic yogurt from a natural food store	1
2 tbsp	coconut oil, melted	30 mL
1 tsp	soy lecithin	5 mL

Soaking: 4 hours
Preparation: 30 minutes
Fermentation: 8 hours
Equipment: blender, dehydrator or yogurt maker

Makes about 1 1/2 cups (375 mL)

1. *Soaking:* In a bowl, soak cashew nuts in water to cover for 4 hours. Rinse thoroughly and discard soaking water.

2. In blender, combine cashew nuts, 1 1/4 cups (300 mL) water and agave nectar and blend into a smooth cream.

3. Add yogurt base or already fermented yogurt and blend for a few seconds to incorporate it.

4. Place mixture in a 2-cup (500 mL) Mason-type jar. The jar must be able to stand inside your dehydrator. If not, divide mixture into two smaller jars. Cover mouth of jar with plastic food wrap. Fasten in place with metal jar ring to get an airtight seal. Adhesive tape can be used instead of metal ring.

5. Place in dehydrator at 105°F (41°C) for 8 hours.

6. Place yogurt in blender. Add coconut oil and blend until incorporated. Blend thoroughly and add soy lecithin.

7. Refrigerate yogurt for at least 1 hour until firm.

TIPS

The fundamental principal of yogurt fermentation is to bring the nut milk to a temperature of between 82°F and 105°F (between 28°C and 41°C), depending on the culture (base) chosen. Below this temperature, fermentation will not occur. Above this temperature, the heat will destroy the bacteria.

It is possible to make yogurt without the recommended equipment, in a room where the temperature is at least 82°F (28°C).

Keeps 1 week in the refrigerator in an airtight container.

Dehydration

Meatless Meat Balls

1¼ cups	sunflower seeds	300 mL
2 tbsp	sunflower oil	30 mL
2 tbsp	apple cider vinegar	30 mL
1 tsp	wheat-free tamari sauce	5 mL
⅓ cup	grated carrot	75 mL
⅓ cup	diced celery (1 to 2 stalks)	75 mL
1 tsp	Garlic Purée (page 25) or 1 clove garlic	5 mL
⅓ cup	finely chopped onion	75 mL
¼ cup	chopped parsley	60 mL
3 tbsp	chopped dried chives	45 mL
3 tbsp	nutritional yeast	45 mL
1 tbsp	chili powder	15 mL
½ tsp	sea salt	2 mL
½ tsp	ground black pepper	2 mL
6 tbsp	ground sunflower seeds	90 mL

Soaking: 8 hours
Preparation: 30 minutes
Dehydration: about 12 hours
Equipment: food processor, dehydrator

Makes 22 balls

1. *Soaking:* In a bowl, soak 1¼ cups (300 mL) sunflower seeds in water to cover for 8 hours. Rinse thoroughly and discard soaking water.

2. In food processor, combine sunflower seeds, oil, vinegar and wheat-free tamari sauce and blend into butter. Set aside.

3. In a salad bowl, combine carrot and celery with sunflower butter and remaining ingredients. Blend by hand to form a paste of even consistency.

4. In palm of hand, scoop 1½ tbsp (22 mL) of dough and form into small balls. Oil hands, if necessary.

5. Place balls on dehydrator trays and dehydrate at 105°F (41°C) for 12 hours. The balls should be firm on the outside, but still tender on the inside.

TIPS

Although there are many dehydrators on the market, we recommend the Excalibur for its efficiency and excellent output. The dehydration times given in this book are for an Excalibur. The Excalibur is a rectangular-shaped dehydrator. There are also ring-shaped ones available but be aware that the time of dehydration might change and the quantities will have to be spread differently.

Keeps 5 to 7 days in the refrigerator in an airtight container.

Living Falafel

3 tbsp	sesame seeds	45 mL
1 cup	walnuts	250 mL
1 cup	unpeeled almonds	250 mL
1/3 cup	sesame seeds, ground	75 mL
2 tbsp	freshly squeezed lemon juice	30 mL
1 tbsp	chopped jalapeño pepper or 1/2 tsp (2 mL) ground cayenne pepper	15 mL
1/2 cup	chopped fresh packed parsley (leaves and stems)	125 mL
1/2 cup	chopped fresh packed cilantro (leaves and stems)	125 mL
1 tbsp	chopped mint	15 mL
1 tbsp	Garlic Purée (page 25) or 2 cloves garlic	15 mL
1/4 cup	olive oil	60 mL
2 tsp	ground oregano	10 mL
1 1/2 tsp	ground cumin	7 mL
1 tsp	sea salt	5 mL
1 tsp	nutritional yeast	5 mL
1/2 tsp	ground black pepper	2 mL

Soaking: 8 hours
Preparation: 30 minutes
Dehydration: about 10 hours
Equipment: food processor, dehydrator

Makes 18 falafels

1. *Soaking:* In a bowl, soak 3 tbsp (45 mL) sesame seeds, walnuts and unpeeled almonds in water to cover for 8 hours. Rinse thoroughly and discard soaking water.

2. In food processor, combine all ingredients except seeds and nuts and purée to an even consistency.

3. Add seeds and nuts and blend until they are all reduced to pieces the size of sesame seeds.

4. Use 3 tbsp (45 mL) each of the mixture to make falafel balls. Flatten balls in the palms of your hands and place directly on dehydrator trays in a single layer and dehydrate at 105°F (41°C) for 10 hours. Turn partway through. Falafels should be dry and slightly crisp on the outside and still moist on the inside.

TIP

Keeps 5 to 7 days in the refrigerator in an airtight container.

Tortillas

1⅓ cups	coarsely chopped red bell pepper	325 mL
1¼ cups	corn kernels, raw, fresh or frozen (if frozen, drain thoroughly after thawing)	300 mL
1¼ cups	coarsely chopped peeled zucchini (1 medium)	300 mL
1½	medium carrots, peeled, coarsely chopped	1½
3 tbsp	olive oil	45 mL
1 tbsp	freshly squeezed lemon juice	15 mL
1½ tsp	chili powder	7 mL
1 tsp	ground cumin	5 mL
½ tsp	sea salt	2 mL
½ cup	ground flax seeds	125 mL

Preparation: 30 minutes

Dehydration: about 7 hours

Equipment: blender, dehydrator, nonstick dehydrator sheets

Makes 15 tortillas

1. In blender, combine all ingredients except flax seeds and blend into a smooth, liquid purée.

2. Pour mixture into a bowl and mix in flax seeds by hand. Let stand for 20 minutes to give flax time to form mucilage.

3. Using a large spoon, in 3 tbsp (45 mL) portions, drop mixture onto nonstick dehydrator sheets, leaving ample space between. Mixture should be liquid but remain in place on the sheets. If necessary, add up to ½ cup (125 mL) ground flax seeds.

4. With a spatula, preferably angled, spread into tortillas measuring 6 inches (15 cm) in diameter.

5. Place sheets in dehydrator and dehydrate at 105°F (41°C) for 4 to 5 hours or until tortillas are firm enough to handle.

6. When they are firm enough, flip over and dehydrate again at 105°F (41°C) for 2 to 3 hours or until both sides are equally dry. Tortillas should be soft and fold without breaking.

TIP

Keeps 2 weeks in the refrigerator in an airtight container with parchment paper separating the tortillas.

Tortilla Chips

6 tbsp	whole dried rosemary, divided	90 mL
½ cup	coarsely chopped red onion	125 mL
4 cups	water	1 L
1½ cups	sun-dried tomatoes	375 mL
3 tbsp	apple cider vinegar	45 mL
1½ tsp	sea salt	7 mL
½ tsp	garlic powder	2 mL
¼ tsp	ground black pepper	1 mL
¼ tsp	ground cayenne pepper	1 mL
2½ cups	ground flax seeds	625 mL

Preparation: 45 minutes
Dehydration: 16 hours
Equipment: blender, dehydrator, nonstick dehydrator sheets

Makes 160 tortilla chips

1. Using a rolling pin or mortar and pestle, coarsely grind half of the rosemary. Set aside.

2. In blender, combine remaining rosemary and all other ingredients except ground flax seeds and purée to an even consistency.

3. Transfer to a bowl and mix in ground flax and rosemary.

4. Place 1 cup (250 mL) of the mixture on a nonstick dehydrator sheet and use a spatula to form a flat, uniform surface.

5. Lightly tracing lines with spatula, divide mixture into 4-inch (10 cm) squares, then cut in half to make 32 triangles.

6. Repeat procedure for each sheet.

7. Place trays in dehydrator and dehydrate at 105°F (41°C) for 16 hours. Turn partway through the cycle, about 8 hours, until firm enough to handle. Tortilla chips are ready when they are completely dry and crunchy.

TIP

Keeps 2 months at room temperature in an airtight container.

Onion Bread

¾ cup	ground flax seeds	175 mL
¾ cup	sunflower seeds, ground	175 mL
1 tsp	dried thyme	5 mL
1 tsp	sea salt	5 mL
⅛ tsp	ground black pepper	0.5 mL
1	clove garlic or 1 tsp (5 mL) Garlic Purée (page 25)	1
1	medium yellow onion, slivered, preferably with a mandoline	1
2 tbsp	sunflower oil	30 mL
½ cup	water	125 mL

Preparation: 35 minutes

Dehydration: about 16 hours

Equipment: large rectangular dehydrator, nonstick dehydrator sheet, mandoline

Makes 32 triangles

1. In a large container, blend all dry ingredients.

2. Mix in moist ingredients (garlic, onion and oil), then add water and blend by hand to obtain a mixture of even consistency.

3. Place a nonstick dehydrator sheet on a cutting board or work surface covered with parchment paper.

4. Spread mixture on dehydrator sheet tray. Use a spatula, preferably angled, or hands to level out dough. To simplify spreading, cover dough with another nonstick dehydrator sheet (or parchment paper) and use a rolling pin to spread dough over entire sheet tray. Use spatula to lift parchment off dough and to flatten out surface.

5. Lightly tracing lines with spatula, divide mixture into 4-inch (10 cm) squares, then cut in half to make 32 triangles.

6. Place sheets in dehydrator and dehydrate at 105°F (41°C) for 16 hours. Turn partway through the cycle, about 8 hours. Triangles should be dry, but not crumbling, and the pieces of onion should still be tender.

TIP

Keeps 3 weeks in the refrigerator in an airtight container.

Pizza Crust

8 cups	Sprouted Buckwheat (page 24), moist or dehydrated	2 L
2 cups	coarsely chopped onion	500 mL
1 1/2 cups	ground flax seeds	375 mL
1 1/2 cups	coarsely chopped peeled zucchini (1 medium)	375 mL
2	cloves garlic or 1 tbsp (15 mL) Garlic Purée (page 25)	2
3/4 cup	sun-dried tomatoes	175 mL
1/3 cup	flax seeds	75 mL
1/3 cup	olive oil	75 mL
2 tbsp	dried marjoram	30 mL
1 1/2 tbsp	ground sage	22 mL
1 tbsp	psyllium	15 mL
1 tbsp	dried chives	15 mL
1 tbsp	dried oregano	15 mL
1 tsp	garlic powder	5 mL
1/2 tsp	sea salt	2 mL
1/4 tsp	ground cayenne pepper	1 mL

Preparation: 40 minutes
Dehydration: about 13 hours
Equipment: food processor, dehydrator

Makes 16 pizza crusts

1. In food processor, combine all ingredients and blend into an even consistency. Blend in 3 or 4 batches, as necessary. If using dehydrated buckwheat, add 1 cup (250 mL) water, as needed to make a spreadable dough.

2. Spread 2 cups (500 mL) of the mixture on a dehydrator mesh sheet. Use a spatula, preferably angled, or hands to level out dough. To simplify spreading, cover dough with a nonstick dehydrator sheet (or parchment paper) and use a rolling pin to spread mixture over entire tray. Use spatula to lift dehydrator sheet off mixture and to flatten out surface.

3. Place tray in dehydrator and dehydrate at 105°F (41°C) for about 12 hours.

4. Turn, lay on tray and return to dehydrator for about 1 hour, until both sides are completely dry.

TIP

Keeps 1 month in the refrigerator in an airtight container.

Sweet Crêpes

2 cups	Brazil nuts	500 mL
3 cups	chopped fresh or frozen bananas	750 mL
2 tbsp	olive oil	30 mL
1 tsp	alcohol-free vanilla essence	5 mL
¼ tsp	ground nutmeg	1 mL
⅛ tsp	sea salt	0.5 mL
½ cup	water, if using fresh bananas	125 mL
⅔ cup	water, if using frozen bananas	150 mL

Preparation: 20 minutes

Dehydration: 8 to 10 hours

Equipment: food processor, blender, dehydrator, nonstick dehydrator sheets

Makes 8 crêpes

1. In food processor, purée Brazil nuts to a liquid, creamy butter, if possible.

2. In blender, combine remaining ingredients and blend to a liquid of even consistency.

3. Add Brazil nut butter to blender and blend again to obtain a smooth mixture of even consistency.

4. Spread ½ cup (125 mL) of the batter on a nonstick dehydrator sheet.

5. With a spatula, preferably angled, spread batter into a crêpe of uniform thickness and about 9 inches (23 cm) in diameter. Repeat until all batter is used up.

6. Place nonstick sheets in dehydrator and dehydrate at 105°F (41°C) for 8 to 10 hours. When they are firm enough to handle, turn as soon as possible onto mesh trays and dehydrate 5 to 6 hours more. Crêpes should be dry to the touch on both surfaces, but remain moist enough to be rolled up without breaking.

TIPS

Although there are many dehydrators on the market, we recommend the Excalibur for its efficiency and excellent output. The dehydration times given in this book are for an Excalibur. The Excalibur is a rectangular-shaped dehydrator. There are also ring-shaped ones available but be aware that the time of dehydration might change and the quantities will have to be spread differently.

Keeps 2 weeks in the refrigerator in an airtight container, with a sheet of parchment paper between each crêpe.

Savory Crêpes

1¼ cups	Brazil nuts	300 mL
7 tbsp	sunflower oil	105 mL
1½ cups	water	375 mL
4 tsp	nutritional yeast	20 mL
1½ tsp	sea salt	7 mL
¾ cup	ground chia seeds	75 mL
¾ cup	ground flax seeds	75 mL

Preparation: 20 minutes
Dehydration: 8 to 10 hours
Equipment: blender, dehydrator, nonstick dehydrator sheets

Makes 8 crêpes

1. In blender, combine all ingredients except ground chia and flax seeds and blend to a liquid of even consistency.

2. Pour into a salad bowl and add ground seeds by hand. Knead until mixture is of even consistency.

3. Place ½ cup (125 mL) of batter on a dehydrator sheet.

4. With a spatula, preferably angled, spread batter into a crêpe of uniform thickness and about 9 inches (23 cm) in diameter. Moisten spatula as needed. Repeat with remaining dough.

5. Place in dehydrator and dehydrate at 105°F (41°C) for 8 to 10 hours. When they are firm enough to handle, turn as soon as possible onto mesh trays and dehydrate 5 to 6 hours more. Crêpes should be dry to the touch on both surfaces, but remain moist enough to be rolled without breaking.

TIP

Keeps 2 weeks in the refrigerator in an airtight container, with a sheet of parchment paper between each crêpe.

Mediterranean Almond Bread

1 cup	chopped sun-dried tomatoes	250 mL
2¼ cups	coarsely chopped apples (2 medium)	550 mL
4 cups	coarsely chopped peeled zucchini (3 medium)	1 L
3 tbsp	freshly squeezed lemon juice	45 mL
½ cup	olive oil	125 mL
1 tsp	sea salt	5 mL
2½ tbsp	fresh or dried basil	37 mL
2 tbsp	fresh or dried parsley	30 mL
2 tbsp	fresh or dried thyme	30 mL
1½ tbsp	fresh or dried oregano	22 mL
⅛ tsp	ground cayenne pepper	0.5 mL
3 cups	finely ground almonds	750 mL
1 cup	ground flax seeds	250 mL
½ cup	sesame seeds	125 mL

Preparation: 40 minutes
Dehydration: 8 to 10 hours
Equipment: food processor, dehydrator, nonstick dehydrator sheets

Makes 25 slices

1. In food processor, combine sun-dried tomatoes, apples, zucchini, lemon juice, olive oil, sea salt and spices and purée to an even consistency.

2. Add ground almonds and blend to obtain a batter of even consistency.

3. Place batter in a bowl and mix in ground flax seeds and sesame seeds by hand.

4. Place batter in blender, 2 cups (500 mL) at a time, and blend.

5. Spread batter on a mesh sheet. Use a spatula, preferably angled, or hands to level out batter. To simplify spreading, cover dough with a nonstick dehydrator sheet (or parchment paper) and use a rolling pin to spread batter over entire tray. Use spatula to lift dehydrator sheet off mixture and to flatten out surface.

6. With a butter knife or spatula, trace separations on each sheet of mixture to form 9 slices of bread, 3 inches (7.5 cm) square.

7. Place on mesh sheets in dehydrator and dehydrate at 105°F (41°C) for about 4 hours. When bread slices are firm enough to handle and can be removed easily from dehydrator sheets, flip them directly onto dehydrator trays, and dehydrate for another 4 hours.

TIP
Keeps 10 days in the refrigerator in an airtight container.

Chapatis

2½ cups	Sprouted Buckwheat (page 24), dehydrated, ground	625 mL
2 cups	ground sunflower seeds	500 mL
1½ cups	ground chia seeds	375 mL
1 cup	ground flax seeds	250 mL
¼ cup	ground sage	60 mL
1 tbsp	sea salt	15 mL
1 tbsp	ground cumin	15 mL
1 tsp	ground black pepper	5 mL
2 cups	water	500 mL
⅔ cup	olive oil	150 mL

Preparation: 45 minutes
Dehydration: about 5 hours
Equipment: dehydrator

Makes 30 chapatis

1. In a large container, blend all dry ingredients.

2. Add water and oil, then blend by hand to form a dough of even consistency.

3. Using an ice cream scoop, divide dough into 30 equal balls.

4. Place balls, one at a time, on a work surface and cover with a nonstick dehydrator sheet or plastic food wrap. Use a rolling pin to flatten balls into thin patties 4 inches (10 cm) in diameter.

5. Place 9 patties on each tray of dehydrator and dehydrate at 105°F (41°C) for 5 hours. Chapatis are ready when they are firm and tender.

TIP

Keeps 2 weeks in the refrigerator in an airtight container.

Kale Chips

Marinade

1½ cups	cashew nuts	375 mL
¾ cup	water	175 mL
¼ cup	wheat-free tamari sauce	60 mL
¼ cup	freshly squeezed lemon juice	60 mL
¼ cup	apple cider vinegar	60 mL
2 tbsp	olive oil	30 mL
1 tbsp	agave nectar	15 mL
¼ cup	nutritional yeast	60 mL
1 tsp	sea salt	5 mL
½ tsp	Garlic Purée (page 25) or ½ clove garlic	2 mL
⅛ tsp	ground cayenne pepper	0.5 mL

Chips

40	leaves kale	40

Soaking: 4 hours
Preparation: 30 minutes
Dehydration: 12 hours
Equipment: blender, dehydrator

Makes 8 cups (2 L) chips

1. *Marinade:* In a bowl, soak cashew nuts in water to cover for 4 hours. Rinse thoroughly and discard soaking water.

2. In blender, combine all marinade ingredients including soaked cashew nuts and blend to a smooth, evenly consistent mixture. Let stand in refrigerator for at least 1 hour and ideally overnight.

3. *Chips:* Remove the long stem that runs up through the kale leaves almost to the top of the plant. Use only the leafy green parts. If some leaves are larger than the palm of your hand, cut them in half. If not, it is important to keep the leaves large, as they will shrink a lot during dehydration. Save stems for a juice recipe that uses kale.

4. In a large container, combine kale leaves and marinade. Mix together thoroughly by hand to soak each leaf.

5. Spread mixture on 9 dehydrator trays in a single layer and dehydrate at 105°F (41°C) for about 12 hours or until dry and crisp.

Beet Crackers

3 cups	pumpkin seeds	750 mL
6 cups	ground flax seeds	1.5 L
3 cups	ground sunflower seeds	750 mL
1 cup	chia seeds	250 mL
2 tbsp	sea salt	30 mL
1½ tbsp	ground black pepper	22 mL
¼ tsp	ground cayenne pepper	1 mL
5	medium carrots, grated	5
2	medium beets, grated	2
2	medium onions, reduced to purée in food processor or blender	2
½ cup	packed chopped fresh parsley (leaves and stems)	125 mL
3	cloves garlic or 1½ tbsp (22 mL) Garlic Purée (page 25)	3
6 tbsp	psyllium	90 mL
4 cups	water	1 L

Soaking: 8 hours
Preparation: 55 minutes
Dehydration: 24 hours
Equipment: blender or food processor, dehydrator

Makes 250 crackers

1. *Soaking:* In a bowl, soak pumpkin seeds in water to cover for 8 hours. Rinse thoroughly and discard soaking water.

2. In a large container, combine ground flax seeds, ground sunflower seeds, chia seeds and spices.

3. Mix in soaked pumpkin seeds and remaining ingredients except water. Add water and knead into a violet-colored mixture of even consistency. Before spreading mixture, let stand 15 minutes to allow mucilage to form. If mixture is too wet when spreading, add up to ¼ cup (60 mL) ground flax seeds.

4. Spread 2 to 2½ cups (500 to 625 mL) of mixture on dehydrator trays. Use a spatula, preferably angled, or hands to level out mixture. To simplify spreading, cover mixture with a nonstick dehydrator sheet (or parchment paper) and use a rolling pin to spread mixture over entire sheet. Use spatula to lift dehydrator sheet off mixture and to flatten out surface.

5. With a butter knife or spatula, lightly trace lines to form 6-inch (15 cm) squares, about 36.

6. Repeat procedure for remaining mixture. If refrigerating mixture to be spread later, it is important to remove it at least 30 minutes before spreading to give it time to soften.

7. Place in dehydrator and dehydrate at 105°F (41°C) overnight.

8. Turn and place on another tray, then dehydrate again until crackers are crisp and completely dry, about 1 day.

TIP

Keeps 4 months at room temperature in an airtight container.

Sun-Dried Tomato Crackers

2 cups	chopped green bell peppers	500 mL
2 cups	packed coarsely chopped fresh cilantro (leaves and stems)	500 mL
5½	medium tomatoes, chopped into large pieces	5½
4 cups	sun-dried tomatoes	1 L
3	cloves garlic or 1 tbsp (15 mL) Garlic Purée (page 25)	3
¼ cup	olive oil	60 mL
4 tsp	sea salt	20 mL
4 cups	ground brown flax seeds	1 L
3 cups	yellow flax seeds	750 mL
2 cups	brown flax seeds	500 mL

Preparation: 1 hour
Dehydration: about 24 hours
Equipment: blender, dehydrator

Makes 300 crackers

1. In blender, combine bell peppers, cilantro, tomatoes, sun-dried tomatoes, garlic, oil and salt and purée to an even consistency.

2. Transfer mixture to a large container and mix in flax seeds by hand. Before spreading mixture, let stand for 15 minutes to allow mucilage to form.

3. Spread 1½ cups (375 mL) of mixture on dehydrator tray, leaving a border. Even out dough using a spatula, preferably angled.

4. With a butter knife or spatula, trace separations on dough to form 6-inch (15 cm) squares, about 36 squares.

5. Repeat procedure for remaining mixture.

6. Place in dehydrator and dehydrate at 105°F (41°C) for about 12 hours.

7. Flip and then dehydrate again until crackers are crisp and completely dry, about 1 day.

TIP

Keeps 4 months at room temperature in an airtight container.

Cranberry and Ginger Granola

½ cup	sunflower seeds	125 mL
½ cup	pumpkin seeds	125 mL
½ cup	sesame seeds	125 mL
1½ cups	dried cranberries	375 mL
½ cup	warm water	125 mL
2 cups	Sprouted Buckwheat (page 24), dehydrated or still moist	500 mL
½ cup	dehydrated ground buckwheat	125 mL
2 cups	shredded coconut	500 mL
⅛ tsp	sea salt	0.5 mL
1½ cups	Date Paste (page 25)	375 mL
1½ tbsp	finely chopped fresh gingerroot	22 mL

Soaking: 8 hours
Preparation: 30 minutes
Dehydration: about 24 hours
Equipment: food processor, dehydrator

Makes 2½ lbs (1.25 kg) granola

1. In a bowl, soak sunflower, pumpkin and sesame seeds in water for 8 hours. Rinse thoroughly and discard soaking water.

2. In another bowl, soak dried cranberries in ½ cup (125 mL) warm water for 15 minutes. In food processor, blend cranberries with their soaking water to reduce to pieces.

3. In a large container, blend buckwheat, ground buckwheat, coconut and salt by hand.

4. Mix in remaining ingredients to form a sticky mixture.

5. Place about 3½ cups (875 mL) of granola on each dehydrator tray and dehydrate at 105°F (41°C) for 16 to 24 hours. Granola is ready when all ingredients are completely dry.

TIP

Keep granola 6 months at room temperature in an airtight container.

Apple and Cinnamon Granola

1 cup	sesame seeds	250 mL
½ cup	sunflower seeds	125 mL
⅓ cup	Sprouted Buckwheat (page 24), dehydrated and ground	75 mL
2 cups	shredded coconut	500 mL
1 cup	chopped dried apples	250 mL
1 cup	sultana raisins	250 mL
1½ cups	Sprouted Buckwheat (page 24), dehydrated or moist	375 mL
4 tsp	ground cinnamon	20 mL
¼ tsp	sea salt	1 mL
1½ cups	Date Paste (page 25)	375 mL

Soaking: 8 hours
Preparation: 30 minutes
Dehydration: about 24 hours
Equipment: dehydrator

Makes 2 lbs (1 kg) granola

1. *Soaking:* In a bowl, soak sesame and sunflower seeds in water to cover for 8 hours. Rinse thoroughly and discard soaking water. Set aside.

2. In a large container, blend all ingredients except date paste. Mix in soaked seeds and date paste by hand.

3. Place about 3½ cups (875 mL) granola on each dehydrator tray and dehydrate at 105°F (41°C) for 16 to 24 hours. Granola is ready when all ingredients are completely dry.

Sufi Nuts

3 cups	unpeeled almonds	750 mL
2 cups	pistachio nuts	500 mL
1½ cups	sesame seeds	375 mL
½ cup	Date Paste (page 25)	125 mL
1 cup	agave nectar	250 mL
1½ tbsp	ground cardamom	22 mL
⅛ tsp	sea salt	0.5 mL
½ cup	finely chopped fresh gingerroot	125 mL
2½ cups	dried cranberries	625 mL

Soaking: 8 hours
Preparation: 30 minutes
Dehydration: about 36 hours
Equipment: blender, dehydrator

Makes 14 cups (3.5 L)

1. *Soaking:* In a bowl, soak almonds, pistachio nuts and sesame seeds in water to cover for 8 hours. Rinse thoroughly and discard soaking water.

2. In a blender, combine date paste, agave nectar, cardamom and salt and blend into a paste of even consistency.

3. Transfer to a large bowl and mix in remaining ingredients including soaked nuts and seeds.

4. Spread about 3 cups (750 mL) of mixture on each dehydrator tray and dehydrate at 105°F (41°C) for about 36 hours. Sufi nuts are ready when they form solid clusters and center of almonds are completely dry.

TIP
Keeps 6 months at room temperature in an airtight container.

Buddha Nuts

3 cups	sunflower seeds	750 mL
3 cups	pumpkin seeds	750 mL
1 1/2 cups	each hazelnuts and almonds	375 mL
1/2 cup	nama shoyu or wheat-free tamari sauce	125 mL
1/4 cup	Date Paste (page 25)	60 mL
2 tbsp	lemon juice	30 mL
1	clove garlic or 1 tsp (5 mL) Garlic Purée (page 25)	1
3 tbsp	paprika	45 mL
3 tbsp	nutritional yeast	45 mL
2 tbsp	dried oregano	30 mL
1 tsp	ground black pepper	5 mL
1/2 tsp	ground cayenne pepper	2 mL

Soaking: 8 hours
Preparation: 30 minutes
Marinating: 6 to 12 hours
Dehydration: about 36 hours
Equipment: dehydrator

Makes 18 cups (4.5 L)

1. *Soaking:* In a bowl, soak sunflower and pumpkin seeds, hazelnuts and unpeeled almonds in water to cover for 8 hours. Rinse thoroughly and discard soaking water.

2. In a large container, blend all ingredients thoroughly including soaked seeds and nuts. Marinate for at least 6 hours or ideally 12 hours in the refrigerator.

3. Spread about 3 cups (750 mL) of mixture on each dehydrator tray without crushing the pieces and keeping close together so clusters form.

4. Place in dehydrator and dehydrate at 105°F (41°C) for about 36 hours. Buddha nuts are ready when they form solid clusters and center of almonds and hazelnuts are completely dry.

TIP

Keeps 6 months at room temperature in an airtight container.

A GIFT FROM THE BEES

The only non-vegan products we use in our restaurants are from bees: honey, pollen and propolis. Pollen is a very good source of essential amino acids and carbohydrates among other nutrients, making it an exceptional superfood. Designated nature's most complete food, pollen is, in fact, a complete plant protein, a source of 22 different minerals and more than a hundred varieties of enzymes. One tablespoonful (15 mL) per day is sufficient to obtain its benefits.

Honey is not used in our kitchens as a sweetener, but rather for its medicinal properties. It is very healing, works as an antibacterial agent and helps your body fend off flu viruses, among other benefits. We recommend you consume it on an empty stomach to obtain the maximum benefits.

Another product from bees that is well worth discovering is propolis. This tree sap is collected by bees, which then coat the walls of the hive with the sap to protect it against bacteria. Propolis can be collected and preserved in alcohol as a tonic for the immune system as well as for clearing the throat. In fact, opera singers do not perform without their vial of propolis in their pocket.

But be warned! The current situation of nature's little workers has become precarious. A large segment of the world's bee population has already been destroyed due to the use of chemicals in agriculture and the fact that some farmers feed the bees with white sugar, weakening their immune systems, thus killing them slowly. Without bees, there is no more pollination and therefore no more flowers, fruits and vegetables! For the producers of bee products, the choice is of capital importance. It is why we recommend using non-pasteurized honey from organic harvests in your region.

Main dishes

Nighttime Pizza

4	Pizza Crusts (page 143)	4
3/4 cup	Sun-Dried Tomato Sauce (page 160)	175 mL
1/2 cup	Kalamata Olive Tapenade (page 116)	125 mL
3/4	medium zucchini, cut into spaghetti with spiral cut machine	3/4
1 cup	arugula	250 mL
	Fennel bulb stems, sliced into thin rounds	
2 tbsp	Crumesan (page 161)	30 mL

Preparation: 5 minutes
Equipment: spiral cut machine

Makes 4 portions

1. On each pizza, spread 3 tbsp (45 mL) Sun-Dried Tomato Sauce and 2 tbsp (30 mL) Kalamata Olive Tapenade. Cover with zucchini spaghetti, then arugula. Top with about 10 slices of fennel.

2. Cut pizzas into four triangular pieces.

3. Sprinkle with Crumesan. Serve cold.

Daytime Pizza

4	Pizza Crusts (page 143)	4
3/4 cup	Caper Aïoli (page 166)	175 mL
4	tomatoes, sliced very thinly with a mandoline	4
24	slices Eggplant Bacon (page 166), cut into small pieces	24
1 cup	shredded spinach	250 mL
1/4 cup	Marinated Vegetables (page 177)	60 mL
1/4 cup	Crème Fraîche (page 175)	60 mL

Preparation: 10 minutes
Equipment: mandoline

Makes 4 portions

1. On each pizza, spread 3 tbsp (45 mL) Caper Aïoli. Then cover with tomato slices, Eggplant Bacon, shredded spinach and drained vegetables.

2. Top each pizza with 1 tbsp (15 mL) crème fraîche.

3. Cut pizzas into four triangular pieces. Serve cold.

Little Quiches

1 tbsp + 1 tsp	Irish moss leaf (see Tips, right)	20 mL
1	recipe Quiche Crust (see right)	1
1/2 cup	vegetables, cut into very small pieces (see Tips, right)	125 mL
1	carrot, peeled, coarsely chopped	1
1/2	medium zucchini, trimmed, coarsely chopped	1/2
1/2 cup	spinach	125 mL
2 tbsp	coarsely chopped onion	30 mL
1/2	clove garlic or 1/2 tsp (2 mL) Garlic Purée (page 25)	1/2
2/3 cup	cashew nuts	150 mL
1/2 cup	water	125 mL
2 tbsp	wheat-free tamari sauce	30 mL
1 tsp	ground turmeric	5 mL
1 tsp	nutritional yeast	5 mL
1/4 tsp	sea salt	1 mL
1/8 tsp	ground black pepper	0.5 mL

Soaking: 36 hours
Preparation: 20 minutes
Equipment: blender

Makes 4 to 6 portions

1. *Soaking:* Thirty-six to 48 hours before you plan to make the quiche, soak Irish moss in cold water then rinse very well. (You should have 2 oz/60 g of soaked Irish moss.) Set aside.

2. Line a small 6-inch (15 cm) pie plate with quiche crust.

3. In large bowl, place the 1/2 cup (125 mL) vegetable mixture. Set aside.

4. In blender, blend remaining ingredients plus reserved soaked Irish moss.

5. Pour contents of vegetables in bowl and blender into quiche crust, then quickly place in refrigerator, uncovered. The Irish moss takes about 3 hours to set completely. During this time, it is important not to move the quiche.

TIPS

Irish moss is available in powder and leaf form. This recipe uses the leaf form. It is available at health food stores or places specializing in herbs.

For the vegetables use onion, cauliflower, bell pepper, zucchini and broccoli.

Garnish quiche with extra vegetables and cashews.

Keeps 4 days in the refrigerator covered with plastic wrap.

Quiche Crust

1/4 cup	chopped sun-dried tomatoes	60 mL
2 tbsp	water	30 mL
3/4 cup	walnuts	175 mL
1/2 cup	Brazil nuts	125 mL
2 tbsp	Sprouted Buckwheat, dehydrated (page 24)	30 mL
1 tbsp	coconut oil, melted	15 mL
1/2	clove garlic or 1/2 tsp (2 mL) Garlic Purée (page 25)	1/2
1/4 tsp	sea salt	1 mL

Soaking: 5 minutes
Preparation: 10 minutes
Equipment: food processor

Makes 1 quiche crust

1. *Soaking:* In a bowl, combine sun-dried tomatoes and water. Let soak while preparing other ingredients.

2. In food processor, blend walnuts, Brazil nuts and buckwheat until nuts are reduced to small bits. The buckwheat will never be completely ground.

3. Drain sun-dried tomatoes and add with remaining ingredients to food processor and blend to a smooth red paste of even consistency.

TIP
Keeps 2 weeks in the refrigerator in an airtight container.

"Pura Vida" Lasagna

2 to 3	medium zucchini, trimmed	2 to 3
2¹⁄₂ cups	Sun-Dried Tomato Sauce (see below)	625 mL
¹⁄₂ cup	fresh basil leaves	125 mL
²⁄₃ cup	Macadamia Ricotta Cheese (page 117)	150 mL
1 tbsp	packed finely chopped parsley leaves	15 mL
1 tbsp	Crumesan (see right)	15 mL

Preparation: 60 minutes
Equipment: mandoline

Makes 8 portions

1. With a mandoline, cut zucchini lengthwise into very thin slices, about $1/16$ inch (2 mm) thick, to form "lasagna noodles."
2. In bottom of an 8-inch (20 cm) square au gratin dish, place zucchini in layers 2 to 3 slices thick and tightly packed together.
3. Top with ¾ cup (175 mL) of tomato sauce.
4. Continue to assemble lasagna by alternating layers of zucchini, ¾ cup (175 mL) of tomato sauce, fresh basil, zucchini, Macadamia Ricotta Cheese (mixed with 1¹⁄₂ tsp/7 mL water if it is too difficult to spread), zucchini, then the remaining tomato sauce. Sprinkle with chopped parsley.
5. Slice carefully with a well sharpened knife and sprinkle each portion with Crumesan.

TIP

Keeps 5 days in the refrigerator in an airtight container

Sun-Dried Tomato Sauce

3	medium tomatoes	3
1¹⁄₄ cups	sun-dried tomatoes	300 mL
1 tbsp	sultana raisins	15 mL
¹⁄₂ cup	coarsely chopped carrot	125 mL
¹⁄₂ cup	coarsely chopped onion	125 mL
1	clove garlic or 1 tsp (5 mL) Garlic Purée (page 25)	1
1¹⁄₂ tsp	olive oil	7 mL
¹⁄₂ tsp	hot pepper flakes	2 mL
¹⁄₂ tsp	dried oregano	2 mL
¹⁄₂ tsp	celery seeds	2 mL
2 tbsp	chopped fresh parsley	30 mL
2 tbsp	chopped fresh basil	30 mL

Preparation: 25 minutes
Equipment: blender

Makes about 2³⁄₄ cups (675 mL)

1. In blender, purée tomatoes. Add sun-dried tomatoes and sultana raisins and let soak in mixture for at least 10 minutes.
2. Blend mixture and add remaining ingredients except fresh parsley and basil. Blend to a sauce with small pieces of vegetable. Add fresh herbs and blend for 5 seconds to incorporate them into the sauce.

TIP

Keeps 10 days in the refrigerator in an airtight container.

Crumesan

1 cup	Brazil nuts	250 mL
1/4 tsp	Garlic Purée (page 25) or 1/4 clove garlic, chopped	1 mL
1/4 tsp	sea salt	1 mL
1/8 tsp	ground black pepper	0.5 mL

Preparation: 5 minutes
Equipment: food processor

Makes about 1 cup (250 mL)

1. In food processor, combine all ingredients and blend briefly by pulsing to a ground but crunchy texture.

TIP

Keeps 2 weeks in the refrigerator in an airtight container.

ÖM Burger

4	Burgers (see below)	4
8	Chapatis (page 147)	8

Toppings, to taste

    Ketchup (page 169)

    Caper Aïoli (page 166)

    Homemade Mustard (see right)

    Lettuce

    Tomato slices

    Slivered onions

    Clover sprouts

Preparation: 5 minutes

Makes 4 portions

1. Spread half the chapatis with ketchup, aïoli and mustard to taste. Then layer remaining halves with lettuce, tomatoes, onions, burger and sprouts. Sandwich together and serve cold.

Burgers

1 cup	sun-dried tomatoes	250 mL
1	medium zucchini, trimmed, coarsely chopped	1
2 cups	coarsely chopped mushrooms	500 mL
1 cup	coarsely chopped onions	250 mL
4	carrots, grated	4
1 cup	coarsely chopped red bell pepper	250 mL
3 tbsp	wheat-free tamari sauce	45 mL
2 tbsp	dried oregano	30 mL
1 tbsp	whole dried rosemary	15 mL
1 tsp	ground black pepper	5 mL
1/8 tsp	ground cayenne pepper	0.5 mL
1 cup	ground flax seeds	250 mL

Preparation: 41 minutes

Dehydration: 6 to 8 hours for "rare"; 8 to 10 hours for "medium-rare"

Equipment: food processor, dehydrator

Makes 10 burgers

1. In a bowl, combine sun-dried tomatoes and a little water. Let soak for 5 minutes, then drain.

2. In food processor, blend all ingredients except ground flax seeds for about 1 minute. Mixture should be of even consistency with small pieces of vegetable.

3. Place mixture in a large container. Add flax seeds. Blend by hand until paste is sticky.

4. Scoop 1/2 cup (125 mL) of mixture for each burger and form by hand or with a mold into burgers 4 inches (10 cm) in diameter. Lay burgers on 2 dehydrator trays and dehydrate at 105°F (41°C) for 6 hours. Turn halfway through cycle. Burgers should hold together but remain soft.

5. To serve warm, dehydrate again at 105°F (41°C) for 20 minutes for "rare" or 1 hour and 30 minutes for "medium rare."

TIP

Keeps 7 days in the refrigerator in an airtight container.

Homemade Mustard

¼ cup	mustard seeds	60 mL
½ cup	apple cider vinegar	125 mL
3 tbsp	olive oil	45 mL
2 tsp	ground sage	10 mL
1 tsp	agave nectar	5 mL
½ tsp	ground turmeric	2 mL
½ tsp	sea salt	2 mL

Soaking: 30 minutes
Preparation: 5 minutes
Equipment: blender

Makes 1 cup (250 mL)

1. *Soaking:* In a bowl, combine mustards seeds and a little water and soak for 30 minutes. Strain seeds to remove as much water as possible. Discard soaking water.

2. In blender, combine seeds and remaining ingredients and blend to a smooth mustard of even consistency. This can take several minutes.

TIPS

For variety, season mustard with your favorite herbs, fruits or spices.

Keeps at least 6 months in the refrigerator in an airtight container.

Spinach Ricotta Portobello Mushrooms

4	portobello mushrooms, trimmed (see Tips, right)	4
¼	recipe Mushroom Marinade (page 47)	¼
½ cup	Macadamia Ricotta Cheese (page 117)	125 mL
1	large handful spinach, chopped	1

Preparation: 10 minutes
Marinating: 1 hour
Dehydration: about 2 hours
Equipment: dehydrator

Makes 4 portions

1. In a large bowl, combine mushrooms and marinade and let stand for about 1 hour.

2. In a bowl, blend together ricotta cheese and chopped spinach. Fill mushrooms with mixture.

3. Place filled mushrooms on dehydrator trays and dehydrate at 105°F (41°C) for 2 hours. The filling will harden, but the entire assembly should remain moist.

TIPS

To clean mushrooms, it is always better to use a basting brush, vegetable brush or cloth. Running them under water saturates them with liquid, reducing their flavor and the appeal of their texture.

Keeps 3 days in the refrigerator in an airtight container.

BLT

24	slices Eggplant Bacon (see below)	24
8	slices Mediterranean Almond Bread (page 146)	8
	Caper Aïoli (see below)	

Toppings, to taste

Lettuce, tomato slices, clover sprouts

Preparation: 5 minutes

Makes 4 portions

1. Cut eggplant bacon into slices ³⁄₄ inch (2 cm) long.

2. Cover slices of bread with aïoli to taste. Top bottom halves with lettuce, tomatoes, sliced eggplant bacon and sprouts. Sandwich together and serve cold.

Eggplant Bacon

1	large eggplant, peeled	1

Marinade

2 tbsp	wheat-free tamari sauce, nama shoyu or Bragg Liquid Aminos	30 mL
2 tbsp	maple syrup	30 mL
2 tsp	olive oil	10 mL
1¹⁄₂ tsp	sun-dried tomatoes	7 mL
¹⁄₄ tsp	chipotle pepper powder	1 mL

Preparation: 20 minutes
Dehydration: 4 to 6 hours
Equipment: mandoline, dehydrator

Makes 30 slices of bacon

1. With mandoline, cut eggplant lengthwise into ¹⁄₈-inch (3 mm) slices.

2. *Marinade:* In a bowl, using a whisk, blend together all ingredients. Place eggplant slices in marinade and blend so they are thoroughly soaked.

3. Spread eggplant slices on 1 or 2 dehydrator trays, being careful to straighten them out and not to overlap them. Dehydrate at 105°F (41°C) for 4 to 6 hours.

TIP

Keeps 2 months in the refrigerator in an airtight container.

Caper Aïoli

2 tbsp	apple cider vinegar	30 mL
2 tbsp	lemon juice	30 mL
2 cups	cashew nuts	500 mL
1	clove garlic or 1 tsp (5 mL) Garlic Purée (page 25)	1
²⁄₃ cup	water	150 mL
1 tsp	salt	5 mL
2 tbsp	packed capers	30 mL

Preparation: 10 minutes
Equipment: blender

Makes 2 cups (500 mL)

1. In blender, combine all ingredients except capers and blend thoroughly into a smooth and creamy sauce.

2. Add capers and blend briefly by pulsing to retain small pieces of caper.

TIP

Keeps 2 weeks in the refrigerator in an airtight container.

Shepherd's Pie

	Lentil Loaf (see below)	
3 cups	corn kernels	750 mL
¼ tsp	sea salt	1 mL
1½ cups	cashew nuts	375 mL
½	medium cauliflower, coarsely chopped	½
2	cloves garlic or 2 tsp (10 mL) Garlic Purée (page 25)	2
¼ cup	olive oil	60 mL
2 tbsp	lemon juice	30 mL
2 tbsp	nutritional yeast	30 mL
1½ tsp	sea salt	7 mL
½ tsp	ground black pepper	2 mL
	Paprika	

Preparation: 30 minutes
Equipment: blender

Makes 15 portions

1. Spread lentil mixture in the bottom of a large au gratin dish.

2. In a bowl, combine corn and salt. Spread corn on top of lentil mixture.

3. In blender, combine remaining ingredients except paprika and blend into a smooth, evenly consistent purée. Spread purée on top of corn. Sprinkle with paprika. Refrigerate for 2 hours to let set.

TIP

Keeps 4 days in the refrigerator in an airtight container.

Lentil Loaf

¾ cup	green, brown or Puy lentils	175 mL
1½ cups	sunflower seeds	375 mL
1 cup	diced red bell pepper	250 mL
2	stalks celery, diced	2
¾ tsp	Garlic Purée (page 25) or 1 small clove garlic	3 mL
¾ cup	slivered onion	175 mL
¼ cup	finely chopped parsley (leaves and stems)	60 mL
1½ tbsp	Bragg Liquid Aminos or nama shoyu	22 mL
2 tbsp	nutritional yeast	30 mL
2 tbsp	sunflower oil	30 mL
2 tbsp	dried chives	30 mL
1 tsp	sea salt	5 mL
½ tsp	ground black pepper	2 mL

Soaking: 12 hours
Preparation: 10 minutes
Sprouting: 1 day

Makes 15 portions

1. *Soaking:* Soak lentils overnight, about 12 hours.

2. In a bowl, cover sunflower seeds with water and soak for 8 hours. Rinse thoroughly and discard soaking water.

3. The next day, rinse lentils well and drain through cheesecloth. A nylon stocking also does the job perfectly. Rinse lentils twice a day until they are sprouted and have doubled in size.

4. In food processor, combine diced pepper and celery and blend for a few seconds to make uniform. Transfer to a bowl and blend with remaining ingredients including drained sunflower seeds and lentils.

TIP

It is important to keep lentils in the dark, at room temperature, for the entire germination period.

Ketchup

2	seedless dates or 2 tbsp (30 mL) Date Paste (page 25)	2
1	medium tomato	1
2 tbsp	olive oil	30 mL
2 tbsp	apple cider vinegar	30 mL
1/2 cup	packed sun-dried tomatoes	125 mL
1/2 tsp	onion powder	2 mL
1/2 tsp	garlic powder	2 mL
1/2 tsp	chili powder	2 mL
1/8 tsp	ground cloves	0.5 mL

Preparation: 10 minutes
Equipment: blender

Makes 2 cups (500 mL)

1. In blender, combine all ingredients and blend to a smooth, evenly consistent red paste. This can take several minutes. If the tomato is very juicy, the ketchup may not be thick enough. In this case, add 2 tbsp (30 mL) sun-dried tomatoes.

TIP
Keeps 3 weeks in the refrigerator in an airtight container.

Mushroom Cannelloni

1½	zucchini, trimmed (approx.)	1½
8	medium spinach leaves	8
½ cup	Macadamia Ricotta Cheese (page 117)	125 mL
	Drained Mushrooms (see below)	
½ cup	Tomato Coulis (see below)	125 mL

Preparation: 15 minutes
Equipment: mandoline

Makes 4 portions

1. With a mandoline, cut zucchini lengthwise into 32 slices thin enough so that they are flexible enough to roll up without breaking.

2. On work surface, lay 4 slices of zucchini, overlapping lengthwise. (They will be rolled up together to form the cannelloni.)

3. On one end of zucchini, place a spinach leaf, letting it extend past one side. Place a ball of 1 tbsp (15 mL) of macadamia ricotta on the spinach leaf. Place 2 tbsp (30 mL) of drained mushrooms on top.

4. Starting from the bottom roll zucchini slices into cannelloni. Repeat procedure with remaining slices.

5. Place 2 tbsp (30 mL) of tomato coulis on a dish and lay 2 cannelloni on top. Repeat with remaining coulis and cannelloni. Serve cold.

Drained Mushrooms

½ cup	sliced mushrooms	125 mL
2 tsp	olive oil	10 mL
1 tsp	sea salt	5 mL
¼ tsp	ground black pepper	1 mL

1. In a salad bowl, combine mushrooms, olive oil, salt and pepper and coat mushrooms thoroughly. Let drain for about 15 minutes. They will reduce in volume by half. Discard water that collects at bottom of bowl before serving. Serve cold.

Tomato Coulis

1	medium tomato	1
¼ cup	packed sun-dried tomatoes	60 mL
2 tbsp	olive oil	30 mL
1 tsp	agave nectar	5 mL
¼ tsp	dried basil or 3 leaves fresh basil	1 mL
¼ tsp	paprika	1 mL
⅛ tsp	cayenne pepper	0.5 mL

Preparation: 5 minutes
Equipment: blender

Makes 1 cup (250 mL)

1. In blender, combine all ingredients and blend to a silky, smooth coulis. If the tomato is very juicy, add up to 2 tbsp (30 mL) sun-dried tomatoes to thicken coulis.

TIP

Keeps 10 days in the refrigerator in an airtight container.

Spinach Pie

1	recipe Pie Crust (page 173)	1
1/2 cup	coarsely chopped sun-dried tomatoes	125 mL
1/2 cup	water	125 mL
2 cups	coarsely chopped spinach	500 mL
1 tbsp	packed finely chopped fresh dill	15 mL
2 tbsp	coconut oil, melted	30 mL
1 tsp	Garlic Purée (page 25) or 1 clove garlic	5 mL
1/4 cup	coarsely chopped red onion	60 mL
1/4 cup	coarsely chopped cauliflower	60 mL
1/2	zucchini, peeled, trimmed (approx.)	1/2
1/2	stalk celery, coarsely chopped	1/2
1/2 cup	cashew nuts	125 mL
1 1/2 tbsp	soy lecithin	22 mL
1 tbsp	nutritional yeast	15 mL
1/2 tsp	sea salt	2 mL
1/4 tsp	ground black pepper	1 mL

Garnish

4 cups	finely chopped spinach	1 L
1/2 cup	packed finely chopped fresh dill	125 mL

Preparation: 20 minutes
Equipment: blender

Makes 8 portions

1. In a bowl, soak sun-dried tomatoes in water. Set aside.

2. Line bottom of 8-inch (20 cm) square au gratin dish with pie crust. Lay chopped spinach and dill on crust.

3. In blender, combine remaining ingredients and sun-dried tomatoes and their soaking water and blend into a liquid of even consistency.

4. Pour mixture into dish. Let set in refrigerator for about 3 hours.

5. Just before serving pie, top with sautéed mushrooms (see below) and garnish with spinach and dill.

Sautéed Mushrooms

3 tbsp	olive oil	45 mL
1 1/2 tsp	balsamic vinegar	7 mL
1/4 tsp	sea salt	1 mL
1/8 tsp	ground black pepper	0.5 mL
2 cups	sliced mushrooms	500 mL

Dehydration: 30 minutes

Makes 2 cups (500 mL)

1. In a bowl, whisk together oil, vinegar, salt and pepper. Add mushrooms and combine thoroughly.

2. Lay mushroom slices on a dehydrator tray and dehydrate at 105°F (41°C) for about 30 minutes.

TIP

Keeps 5 to 7 days in the refrigerator in an airtight container.

Pie Crust

2 tsp	coconut oil, melted	10 mL
2/3 cup	Brazil nuts	150 mL
1/3 cup	walnuts	75 mL
3 tbsp	coarsely chopped sun-dried tomatoes	45 mL
1/4 cup	Sprouted Buckwheat, dehydrated (page 24)	60 mL
1 1/2 tbsp	Ketchup (page 169)	22 mL
1 1/2 tbsp	ground flax seeds	22 mL

Preparation: 10 minutes
Equipment: food processor

Makes 1 crust

1. In food processor, combine all ingredients except ketchup and ground flax seeds and blend to a paste of even consistency, retaining small pieces of nut.

2. In a bowl, blend together Brazil nut mixture with ketchup and flax seeds.

TIP

Keeps 2 weeks in the refrigerator in an airtight container.

Supreme Tacos

8	leaves lettuce	8
8	Tortillas (page 140)	8
16	Meatless Meat Balls (page 138), quartered	16
8 tbsp	Chipotle Sauce (page 109)	120 mL
1	avocado, thinly sliced	1
¼	red bell pepper, julienned	¼
8	branches fresh cilantro	8
½ cup	clover sprouts	125 mL
	Crème Fraîche (see right)	
¼	recipe Salsa (see right)	¼

Preparation: 5 minutes

Makes 4 portions

1. Place 1 leaf of lettuce in each tortilla. On lettuce, place 8 pieces of meat ball and top with 1 tbsp (15 mL) of chipotle sauce.

2. Place avocado slices, julienned bell pepper and 1 branch of cilantro lengthwise on lettuce. Top with a large handful of clover sprouts.

3. Add dollops of crème fraîche before closing taco. Serve with salsa. Serve cold.

Salsa

1	tomato, diced very small	1
¼ cup	diced zucchini	60 mL
2 tbsp	fresh cilantro	30 mL
1 tbsp	finely chopped red onion	15 mL
	Juice of ¼ lemon or ¼ lime	
½ tsp	olive oil	2 mL
½ tsp	sea salt	2 mL
⅛ tsp	ground cayenne pepper or some diced jalapeño pepper	0.5 mL

Preparation: 10 minutes

Makes about 1 cup (250 mL)

1. In a bowl, combine all ingredients and blend together.

TIP

Keeps 1 week in the refrigerator in an airtight container.

Crème Fraîche

1 cup	cashew nuts	250 mL
⅓ cup	freshly squeezed lemon juice	75 mL
1 tsp	sea salt	5 mL

Soaking: 4 hours
Preparation: 10 minutes
Equipment: blender

Makes about 1 cup (250 mL)

1. *Soaking:* In a bowl, soak cashew nuts with water for 4 hours. Rinse thoroughly and discard soaking water.

2. In blender, combine all ingredients, including soaked cashew nuts, and blend to a creamy, smooth sauce of even consistency.

3. For a more liquid crème fraîche, add 2 tbsp (30 mL) water.

TIPS

It is possible to make this recipe without soaking the nuts. In this case, add ¼ cup (60 mL) water.

Keeps 1 week in the refrigerator in an airtight container.

Crêpes Florentine

4	Savory Crêpes (page 144)	4
³/₄ cup	Cashew Nut Cheese (page 125)	175 mL
2	large handfuls spinach, cut into thin strips	2
¹/₂ cup	sun-dried tomatoes	125 mL
8	fresh basil leaves	8
	Marinated Vegetables (see below)	
4 tbsp	Crème Fraîche (page 175)	60 mL

Preparation: 10 minutes

Makes 4 portions

1. Spread nut cheese equally on each crêpe. Top with spinach and sun-dried tomatoes. Add basil and marinated vegetables to taste.

2. Roll up crêpes, then place 1 tbsp (15 mL) of crème fraîche on each one.

Marinated Vegetables

¹/₂ cup	sliced mushrooms	125 mL
¹/₂ cup	julienned zucchini	125 mL
¹/₂ cup	broccoli florets	125 mL
¹/₂ cup	julienned red bell pepper	125 mL
¹/₄ cup	sliced rounds red onion	60 mL

Marinade

2 tbsp	olive oil	30 mL
2 tbsp	nama shoyu	30 mL
1 tbsp	apple cider vinegar	15 mL
¹/₂ tsp	ground black pepper	2 mL

Makes about 1 cup (250 mL)

1. In a salad bowl, combine vegetables.

2. *Marinade:* In a small bowl, combine all ingredients. Add to vegetables in bowl and soak vegetables in marinade for about 15 minutes. Serve cold.

Optional

Dehydrate vegetables at 105°F (41°C) for 1 hour.

Crêpes Botanical

4	Savory Crêpes (page 144)	4
³/₄ cup	Pistachio Basil Pesto (page 121)	175 mL
2	medium tomatoes, each cut into 6 round slices	2
2	large handfuls arugula	2
¹/₄ cup	capers	60 mL
8	thin rounds red onion	8
4 tbsp	Crème Fraîche (page 175)	60 mL

Preparation: 10 minutes

Makes 4 portions

1. Spread pesto equally on each crêpe. Top with tomatoes, arugula, capers and onion.

2. Roll up, then place 1 tbsp (15 mL) of crème fraîche on each crêpe. Serve cold.

Pesto Spaghetti

1	apple	1
8	zucchini (approx.)	8
¾ cup	Pistachio Basil Pesto (page 121)	175 mL
2 tbsp	freshly squeezed lemon juice	30 mL
2 tbsp	olive oil	30 mL
6	large handfuls of spinach	6
1 cup	Marinated Mushrooms (see below)	250 mL
¼ cup	Crumesan (page 161)	60 mL

Optional

16	Meatless Meat Balls (page 138)	16

Preparation: 10 minutes

Equipment: spiral cut machine or mandoline

Makes 4 portions

1. Using spiral cut machine or mandoline, cut apple and zucchini into spaghetti.

2. In a salad bowl, combine spaghetti, pesto, lemon juice and olive oil.

3. Lay a bed of spinach on each dish. Top with a scoop of spaghetti with pesto, marinated mushrooms and meatless meat balls, if using. Sprinkle with Crumesan. Serve cold.

Marinated Mushrooms

2 cups	sliced mushrooms	500 mL
4 tsp	olive oil	20 mL
4 tsp	sea salt	20 mL
1 tsp	ground black pepper	5 mL

Makes 1 cup (250 mL)

1. In a salad bowl, combine mushrooms, olive oil, salt and pepper and coat mushrooms thoroughly. Let drain for about 15 minutes. They will reduce in volume by half.

2. Discard water that collects at bottom of bowl before serving. Serve cold.

Pad Thai

Vegetable Mixture

1¹/₂	zucchini, cut into spaghetti with spiral cut machine or mandoline (approx.)	1¹/₂
1	medium daikon (giant white Japanese radish), cut into spaghetti	1
1 cup	shredded red cabbage	250 mL
1 cup	julienned red bell pepper	250 mL
1 cup	julienned yellow bell pepper	250 mL
¹/₄ cup	chopped green onion	60 mL
2 cups	sunflower sprouts	500 mL
¹/₂ cup	chopped packed fresh cilantro (leaves and stems)	125 mL
¹/₂ cup	Pad Thai sauce (see below)	125 mL
¹/₂ cup	coarsely chopped cashew nuts	125 mL
¹/₂	lime, cut into 4 wedges	¹/₂
	Whole fresh cilantro leaves	

Preparation: 20 minutes
Equipment: spiral cut machine or mandoline

Makes 4 portions

1. *Vegetable Mixture:* In a bowl, combine all ingredients. Add Pad Thai sauce and blend thoroughly.

2. Place a mound of mixture on each dish. Sprinkle with chopped cashew nuts. Garnish with a wedge of lime and fresh whole cilantro leaves. Serve cold.

Pad Thai Sauce

¹/₄ cup	tamarind paste	60 mL
¹/₄ cup	agave nectar	60 mL
¹/₄ cup	wheat-free tamari sauce	60 mL
¹/₄ cup	sunflower oil	60 mL
2 tbsp	hot pepper flakes	30 mL
2 tbsp	water	30 mL
1 tbsp	Garlic Purée (page 25) or 2 cloves garlic	15 mL

Preparation: 5 minutes
Equipment: blender

Makes 2 cups (500 mL)

1. In blender, combine all ingredients and blend to a thick sauce.

TIP
Keeps 2 weeks in the refrigerator in an airtight container.

Teriyaki Brochette

8	wooden chopsticks	8
1	medium zucchini, sliced into half moons	1
1	red onion, cut into 16 triangles	1
1	red bell pepper, cut into cubes	1
16	Meatless Meat Balls (page 138)	16
8	mushrooms, brushed, stems removed	8
1	yellow bell pepper, cut into cubes	1
	Teriyaki Orange Sauce (see below)	

Preparation: 20 minutes
Marinating: 1 to 8 hours
Dehydration: 45 minutes
Equipment: dehydrator

Makes 4 portions

1. On each wooden chopstick, spear a half moon of zucchini, a triangle of red onion, a square of red bell pepper, a meatless meat ball, a mushroom, a square of yellow bell pepper, another triangle of red onion and another half moon of zucchini.

2. Using a basting brush, brush brochettes with a generous amount of teriyaki sauce and marinate in refrigerator for at least 1 hour or ideally for 8 hours.

3. Place in dehydrator at 105°F (41°C) and dehydrate for 45 minutes. It is preferable to serve warm.

TIP

Keeps 5 days in the refrigerator in an airtight container.

Teriyaki Orange Sauce

1/2 cup	wheat-free tamari sauce	125 mL
2	seedless dates or 2 tbsp (30 mL) Date Paste (page 25)	2
1	clove garlic or 1 tsp (5 mL) Garlic Purée (page 25)	1
1 1/2 tbsp	chopped ginger or 1 1/2 tsp (7 mL) Ginger Juice (page 24)	22 mL
1 tbsp	orange juice	15 mL
1/4 tsp	lemon juice	1 mL
1/4 tsp	orange essence	1 mL
1/4 tsp	sesame oil (see Tips, right)	1 mL
1/8 tsp	ground cayenne pepper	0.5 mL

Preparation: 10 minutes
Equipment: blender

Makes about 3/4 cup (175 mL)

1. In blender, combine all ingredients and blend to a sauce of even consistency.

TIPS

If you're following a completely raw food diet, look for untoasted sesame oil that is completely unrefined with the label "cold-pressed."

Keeps 2 weeks in the refrigerator in an airtight container.

Desserts

Ginger Snaps

1/3 cup	coarsely chopped unpeeled ginger	75 mL
1 cup	coconut sugar	250 mL
2 1/2 cups	water	625 mL
1/2 cup	ground flax seeds	125 mL
3 cups	fresh nut pulp (pulp that remains in filter after making a nut milk)	750 mL
1 tsp	ground cinnamon	5 mL
1/8 tsp	sea salt	0.5 mL

Preparation: 15 minutes
Dehydration: about 20 hours
Equipment: blender, dehydrator, nonstick dehydrator sheet

Makes 35 cookies

1. In blender, combine ginger, sugar and water and blend to a smooth, evenly consistent mixture.

2. Add ground flax seeds and blend again to thoroughly incorporate.

3. Place mixture in a bowl and add nut pulp, cinnamon and sea salt. Blend to obtain a sticky paste of even consistency.

4. Form into balls using 2 tbsp (30 mL) of mixture for each. Place on a nonstick dehydrator sheet and flatten slightly with the back of a spoon to form cookies of about 3 inches (7.5 cm) in diameter.

5. Place in dehydrator and dehydrate at 105°F (41°C) for 15 hours.

6. Turn cookies and place on racks in dehydrator. Dehydrate for 5 hours to dry them evenly. They should be completely dry and crispy.

TIP

Keeps 2 weeks in the refrigerator in an airtight container.

Macadamia Nut Cookies

1 cup	macadamia nuts	250 mL
1 1/2 cups	Date Paste (page 25)	375 mL
1 1/2 tsp	Ginger Juice (page 24) or 1 1/2 tsp (7 mL) chopped ginger	7 mL
2 tbsp	sunflower oil	30 mL
2 cups	shredded coconut	500 mL
1 cup	Sprouted Buckwheat, dehydrated (page 24)	250 mL
1 1/3 cups	currants	325 mL
1 tbsp	alcohol-free vanilla essence	15 mL
1/2 tsp	maca powder	2 mL
1/4 tsp	sea salt	1 mL

Preparation: 15 minutes
Dehydration: about 12 hours
Equipment: food processor, dehydrator

Makes 30 cookies

1. In food processor, coarsely chop macadamia nuts for a few seconds.

2. In a large bowl, combine macadamia nut pieces and remaining ingredients and blend to an evenly consistent paste.

3. Form cookies using 1/4 cup (60 mL) of mixture for each.

4. Place on three racks in dehydrator and dehydrate at 105°F (41°C) for about 12 hours. Cookies should be dry, but not breakable, and still moist inside.

TIP

Keeps 2 weeks in the refrigerator in an airtight container.

Chocolate Mousse

1/3 cup	cocoa butter	75 mL
1/4 cup	coconut oil	60 mL
4 1/2 cups	water	1.125 L
3 cups	grated coconut	750 mL
1 1/2 cups	cocoa powder	375 mL
2/3 cup	agave nectar	150 mL
2 tsp	alcohol-free vanilla essence	10 mL

Preparation: 15 minutes
Equipment: blender, dehydrator

Makes 8 portions

1. Melt cocoa butter and coconut oil in the dehydrator or a bain-marie. If using a bain-marie, stir constantly so the temperature does not exceed 105°F (41°C).

2. During this time, prepare a milk with water and grated coconut (see Nut Milks, page 21). Use 3 1/2 cups (875 mL) of the milk for the mousse.

3. Add coconut milk to blender with cocoa powder, agave nectar and vanilla essence and blend to a smooth and even consistency.

4. Add melted cocoa butter and coconut oil mixture slowly to the blender, mixing at low speed for several seconds so the chocolate does not separate.

5. Pour into a container and let set in the refrigerator for about 3 hours.

TIPS

Keeps 7 days in the refrigerator in an airtight container.

Serve with Raspberry Coulis (see below), if desired.

Raspberry Coulis

2 cups	raspberries	500 mL
2 tbsp	agave nectar	30 mL

Preparation: 5 minutes
Equipment: blender

Makes 1 cup (250 mL)

1. In blender, combine both ingredients and crush for several minutes to make all the raspberry seeds disappear.

2. If using frozen raspberries that have not been previously thawed, add 1/4 to 3/4 cup (60 to 175 mL) water to obtain a sufficiently liquid coulis.

TIP

Keeps 1 week in the refrigerator in an airtight container.

Choco-Banana Pie

1	recipe Coco-Macadamia Crust (see below)	1
2 cups	cashew nuts	500 mL
2	medium bananas, reduced to purée in blender	2
1 cup	water	250 mL
1/2 cup	agave nectar	125 mL
1/2 tsp	alcohol-free vanilla essence	2 mL
1/4 cup	carob	60 mL
1/4 cup	cocoa powder	60 mL
1/4 tsp	ground cinnamon	1 mL
1/4 cup	coconut oil, melted	60 mL
2 tbsp	sunflower lecithin or soy lecithin	30 mL

Garnish

30	round slices of fresh or dehydrated banana	30
2 tbsp	raw cacao nibs	30 mL

Preparation: 15 minutes
Equipment: food processor, blender

Makes 10 portions

1. Line bottom and sides of a 9-inch (23 cm) pie plate with crust.
2. In food processor, purée cashew nuts to powder.
3. In blender, combine cashew powder and remaining ingredients except coconut oil and lecithin and blend to a smooth, evenly consistent paste.
4. While blender is running, add melted coconut oil and sunflower lecithin. Blend again for 30 seconds to thoroughly incorporate.
5. Quickly pour mixture into crust, then refrigerate for about 4 hours to allow pie to set. Garnish with bananas and cacao nibs.

TIP

Keeps 10 days in the refrigerator in an airtight container or for up to 4 months in the freezer.

Coco-Macadamia Crust

1/2 cup	macadamia nuts	125 mL
1 cup	shredded coconut	250 mL
2 1/2 tbsp	Date Paste (page 25) or 3 chopped seedless dates	37 mL
1/2 tsp	alcohol-free vanilla essence	2 mL
1/4 tsp	sea salt	1 mL

Preparation: 10 minutes
Equipment: food processor

Makes 1 crust

1. In food processor, chop macadamia nuts to small pieces.
2. Add remaining ingredients and blend to obtain an evenly consistent crust that can be formed into a ball.

TIP

Keeps 2 weeks in the refrigerator in an airtight container.

Island Lime Pie

1	recipe Coco-Macadamia Crust (page 190)	1

Avocado Mousse

	Flesh of 2 to 3 avocados	
³/₄ cup	freshly squeezed lime or lemon juice	175 mL
¹/₂ cup	coconut butter	125 mL
¹/₂ cup	agave nectar	125 mL
¹/₂ tsp	alcohol-free vanilla essence	2 mL

Frosting

¹/₄ cup	water	60 mL
1 tbsp	freshly squeezed lime or lemon juice	15 mL
¹/₂ cup	macadamia nuts	125 mL
2 tsp	agave nectar	10 mL
¹/₄ tsp	alcohol-free vanilla essence	1 mL
¹/₈ tsp	sea salt	0.5 mL
1 tbsp	coconut oil, melted	15 mL

Preparation: 15 minutes
Equipment: blender, food processor, pastry bag

Makes 12 portions

1. Line the bottom and sides of a 9-inch (23 cm) pie plate with crust.

2. *Avocado Mousse:* In food processor, combine all ingredients and blend to a smooth cream of even consistency. Pour into crust. Keep at room temperature while preparing frosting.

3. *Frosting:* In blender, combine all ingredients except melted coconut oil and blend to a smooth cream of even consistency. This can take several minutes. If needed, add 1 to 2 tbsp (15 to 30 mL) more water. While blender is running, incorporate melted coconut oil.

4. Place mixture in a pastry bag with a narrow nozzle.

5. Trace a spiral of frosting on the pie from the center to the rim of the pie plate. With a chopstick, trace a dozen lines in the frosting at regular intervals from the center to the rim to resemble a spider web.

TIPS

Keeps 10 days in the refrigerator in an airtight container or for up to 4 months in the freezer.

Garnish with lime slices and grated coconut, if desired.

Sugar Pie

1	recipe Coco-Pecan Crust (see below)	1
3 cups	Brazil nuts	750 mL
³⁄₄ cup	Date Paste (page 25)	175 mL
3 tbsp	maple syrup	45 mL
1 tsp	alcohol-free vanilla essence	5 mL
¹⁄₈ tsp	sea salt	0.5 mL
¹⁄₃ cup	melted coconut oil	75 mL

Preparation: 15 minutes
Equipment: food processor, blender

Makes 12 portions

1. Line a 9-inch (23 cm) pie plate with crust. The pie plate should preferably have a removable bottom.

2. In food processor, reduce Brazil nuts to a butter that is as liquid and creamy as possible. This can take several minutes.

3. Pour mixture into blender. Add date paste, maple syrup, vanilla essence and salt. Reduce to a smooth paste of even consistency.

4. While blender is running, incorporate melted coconut. Continue blending until mixture is creamy and of even consistency.

5. Pour mixture into crust. Refrigerate pie for 3 hours to allow it to set.

TIPS

Keeps 10 days in the refrigerator in an airtight container or for up to 4 months in the freezer.

Garnish with pecans, if desired.

Coco-Pecan Crust

1¹⁄₂ cups	pecans	375 mL
1 cup	shredded coconut	250 mL
3 tbsp	Date Paste (page 25) or 3 seedless dates, chopped	45 mL
1 tsp	ground cinnamon	5 mL
¹⁄₄ tsp	ground ginger	1 mL
¹⁄₄ tsp	ground cardamom	1 mL
¹⁄₄ tsp	ground cloves	1 mL
¹⁄₄ tsp	ground nutmeg	1 mL
¹⁄₈ tsp	sea salt	0.5 mL

Preparation: 10 minutes
Equipment: food processor

Makes 1 crust

1. In food processor, reduce pecans to powder.

2. Add remaining ingredients and blend into a crust of even consistency that can be formed into a ball. If mixture is not holding together, add up to 1 date or 1 tbsp (15 mL) more date paste.

TIP

Keeps 2 weeks in the refrigerator in an airtight container.

Seasonal Fruit Pie

1 tbsp + 1 tsp	Irish moss leaf (see Tips, right)	20 mL
1	recipe Crispy Crust (see below)	1
	Zest of 2 lemons	
3 tbsp	freshly squeezed lemon juice	45 mL
1 cup	water	250 mL
3/4 cup	cashew nuts	175 mL
1/4 cup	agave nectar	60 mL
1 tsp	alcohol-free vanilla essence	5 mL
1 1/2 tsp	soy lecithin	7 mL
1/8 tsp	sea salt	0.5 mL
1/4 cup	coconut oil, melted	60 mL
	Fresh fruits in season	

Soaking: 36 hours

Makes 12 portions

1. *Soaking:* Thirty-six to 48 hours before you plan to make the fruit pie, soak Irish moss in cold water then rinse very well. (You should have 2 oz/60 g of soaked Irish moss.) Set aside.

2. Line a 9-inch (23 cm) pie plate with crust. Pie plate should preferably have a removable bottom.

3. In blender, combine soaked Irish moss and remaining ingredients except coconut oil and fresh fruits. Blend to a smooth, evenly consistent liquid. While blender is running, incorporate coconut oil.

4. Quickly pour mixture onto pie crust and refrigerate for about 3 hours to allow pie to set. Serve as is or fill with fresh seasonal fruit just before serving.

TIPS

Irish moss is available in powder and leaf form. This recipe uses the leaf form. It is available at health food stores or places specializing in herbs.

Keeps 10 days in the refrigerator covered tightly with plastic wrap or for up to 4 months in the freezer.

Crispy Crust

1 cup	walnuts	250 mL
1/2 cup	Sprouted Buckwheat, dehydrated (page 24)	125 mL
1/4 cup	shredded coconut	60 mL
1/4 cup	coconut sugar	60 mL
1/8 tsp	sea salt	0.5 mL
4	whole seedless dates	4
1 tbsp	Date Paste (page 25)	15 mL
1/4 cup	sultana raisins	60 mL
1/2 tsp	alcohol-free vanilla essence	2 mL

Preparation: 5 minutes
Equipment: food processor

Makes 1 crust

1. In food processor, combine walnuts, dehydrated sprouted buckwheat, shredded coconut, sugar and salt and purée to a fine flour.

2. Add remaining ingredients and blend to a sticky paste. If paste is not holding together, add up to 1 tsp (5 mL) more date paste.

TIP

Keeps 2 weeks in the refrigerator in an airtight container.

"Cheese" Cake

1	recipe Spiced Fig Crust (see below)	1
1⅓ cups	cashew nuts	325 mL
3 tbsp	freshly squeezed lemon juice	45 mL
1⅓ cups	coconut oil, melted	325 mL
2½ cups	Cashew Nut Cheese (page 125)	625 mL
1 cup	agave nectar	250 mL
¼ cup	sunflower lecithin or soy lecithin	60 mL
2 tsp	almond essence	10 mL
1½ tsp	alcohol-free vanilla essence	7 mL
⅛ tsp	sea salt	0.5 mL

Blueberry Coulis

2 cups	blueberries	500 mL
2 tbsp	water	30 mL
2 tbsp	agave nectar	30 mL
2 tbsp	coconut oil, melted	30 mL

Soaking: 4 hours
Preparation: 20 minutes
Equipment: food processor, blender

Makes 18 portions

1. *Soaking:* In a bowl, soak cashew nuts for 4 hours. Rinse thoroughly and discard soaking water.

2. Line a 10-inch (25 cm) springform pan with crust.

3. In food processor, reduce cashew nuts to a powder.

4. In blender, combine cashew nut powder, lemon juice and melted coconut oil and blend to a smooth cream.

5. Add remaining ingredients and blend to a smooth, evenly consistent paste. Pour mixture into pan. Clean edges of pan and keep pie at room temperature while preparing coulis.

6. *Blueberry Coulis:* In blender, combine blueberries, water and agave nectar and blend to a liquid coulis. This can take several minutes if blueberries are frozen. If coulis is too thick, add ¼ to ½ cup (60 to 125 mL) water.

7. While blender is running, incorporate melted coconut oil and continue to blend for a few seconds to obtain even consistency.

8. Pour half of coulis on top of cake. Use a spoon to trace a marble pattern through it. Refrigerate for about 2 to 3 hours to allow pie to harden. Pour remaining coulis into a container and pour on cake just before serving.

TIP
Keeps 10 days in the refrigerator in an airtight container or for up to 4 months in the freezer.

Spiced Fig Crust

1 cup	diced dried figs	250 mL
¾ cup	Brazil nuts	175 mL
¼ tsp	ground nutmeg	1 mL
¼ tsp	ground cinnamon	1 mL
⅛ tsp	sea salt	0.5 mL

Preparation: 5 minutes
Equipment: food processor

Makes 1 crust

1. In food processor, combine all ingredients and blend to a granular crust.

TIP
Keeps 2 weeks in the refrigerator in an airtight container.

Carrot Cake

Cake

3½ cups	ground almonds	875 mL
13	chopped carrots, reduced to purée in blender or food processor (approx.)	13
2 cups	Date Paste (page 25)	500 mL
	Zest of 1 orange	
	Zest of 1 lemon	
1 cup	coconut butter	250 mL
1 tsp	alcohol-free vanilla essence	5 mL
2 tsp	ground cinnamon	10 mL
½ tsp	ground cloves	2 mL
½ tsp	ground ginger	2 mL
½ tsp	sea salt	2 mL
1 cup	walnuts, chopped with a knife	250 mL
1 cup	dried currants	250 mL

Frosting

2 tbsp	coconut butter	30 mL
1 cup	Brazil nuts	250 mL
	Zest and juice of ½ lemon	
	Juice of 1 orange	
1 cup	cashew nuts	250 mL
¼ cup	agave nectar	60 mL
¼ cup	water	60 mL
1 tbsp	sunflower lecithin or soy lecithin	15 mL
1 tsp	alcohol-free vanilla essence	5 mL

Preparation: 41 minutes
Equipment: food processor, blender

Makes 18 portions

1. *Cake:* In food processor, in 2 or 3 batches, if necessary, combine all ingredients except walnuts and currants and blend to a paste of even consistency.

2. Incorporate walnuts and currants by hand.

3. Spread paste into 2 large 10-inch (25 cm) springform pans. Place in freezer while preparing frosting.

4. *Frosting:* In blender, combine all ingredients and blend to a smooth cream of even consistency.

5. Spread frosting on top of 2 cakes and let set in refrigerator for about 2 hours.

6. When cakes have hardened, stack one on top of the other (cake, frosting, cake, frosting) to form a layer cake.

TIPS

Divide this recipe in half to make a single-layer cake of 9 portions.

Keeps 10 days in the refrigerator in an airtight container or for up to 4 months in the freezer.

"Dark Desire" Cake

1	"Dark Desire" Crust (see right)	1

Mousse

1 cup	water	250 mL
³/₄ cup	shredded coconut	175 mL
1 cup	ground hazelnuts	250 mL
1 cup	cashew nuts	250 mL
¹/₂ cup	walnuts	125 mL
¹/₂ cup	Date Paste (page 25)	125 mL
¹/₄ cup	coconut butter	60 mL
¹/₃ cup	cocoa powder	75 mL
3 tbsp	agave nectar	45 mL
¹/₂ tsp	alcohol-free vanilla essence	2 mL
¹/₈ tsp	sea salt	0.5 mL
¹/₂ cup	coconut oil, melted	125 mL
2 tbsp	raw cacao nibs	30 mL

Ganache

2 tbsp	coconut oil, melted	30 mL
¹/₄ tsp	lemon juice	1 mL
¹/₂ cup	shredded coconut	125 mL
¹/₄ cup	agave nectar	60 mL
2 tbsp	sunflower lecithin or soy lecithin	30 mL
¹/₄ cup	water	60 mL
¹/₂ cup	cocoa powder	125 mL
	Chocolate Frosting (page 216)	

Preparation: 25 minutes
Equipment: food processor, blender

Makes 9 portions

1. Line a 9-inch (23 cm) springform pan with crust.
2. *Mousse:* In a bowl, combine water and shredded coconut and make a milk (see Nut Milks, page 21). You will use ¹/₂ cup (125 mL) of milk in this recipe.
3. Pour milk into food processor, then add remaining ingredients except coconut oil and cacao nibs and blend to a smooth paste of even consistency. Add coconut oil and continue blending to incorporate.
4. Add cacao nibs and blend for a few seconds to incorporate them while keeping them whole.
5. Spread mousse on crust. Clean edges of pan thoroughly to avoid staining ganache.
6. *Ganache:* In blender, combine all ingredients except cocoa powder and blend to a paste of even consistency. Add cocoa powder and blend to thoroughly incorporate it.
7. Spread ganache over cake. Refrigerate for about 3 hours to allow it to harden.
8. *Topping:* Cover with Chocolate Frosting.

TIP
Keeps 10 days in the refrigerator in an airtight container or for up to 4 months in the freezer.

"Dark Desire" Crust

1/4 cup	hazelnuts	60 mL
1/4 cup	Brazil nuts	60 mL
1 tbsp	Date Paste (page 25)	15 mL
3 tbsp	shredded coconut	45 mL
1/8 tsp	sea salt	0.5 mL
1 tbsp	raw cacao nibs	15 mL

Preparation: 5 minutes
Equipment: food processor

Makes 1 crust

1. In food processor, combine all ingredients except cacao nibs and blend for several seconds to obtain a crust that is crunchy but evenly consistent. It is important not to blend too much, as this will reduce the Brazil nuts to butter.

2. Add cacao nibs to food processor and blend for a few seconds to incorporate them while keeping them whole.

TIP

Keeps 2 weeks in the refrigerator in an airtight container.

Tiramisu

Soaking

1 tbsp	Irish moss leaf (see Tips, page 197)	15 mL
1/2 cup	unpeeled almonds	125 mL
1 tsp	espresso coffee beans, ground very finely	5 mL
1/2 cup	cashew nuts	125 mL

Cake

1 1/4 cups	almonds, ground	300 mL
1/3 cup	Date Paste (page 25)	75 mL
2 tbsp	coconut oil, melted	30 mL
1 tsp	alcohol-free vanilla essence	5 mL
1/8 tsp	sea salt	0.5 mL

Mocha

2 tbsp	agave nectar	30 mL
2 tbsp	coconut oil, melted	30 mL
1 1/2 tbsp	Date Paste (page 25)	22 mL
1 1/2 tbsp	cocoa powder	22 mL
2 1/4 tsp	alcohol-free vanilla essence	11 mL
1 1/2 tsp	soy lecithin	7 mL
1/8 tsp	sea salt	0.5 mL

Frosting

1/3 cup	coconut oil, melted	75 mL
2 tbsp	agave nectar	30 mL
2 1/4 tsp	soy lecithin	11 mL
1/2 tsp	alcohol-free vanilla essence	2 mL
1/8 tsp	sea salt	0.5 mL
	Cocoa powder	

Soaking: 36 hours
Preparation: 50 minutes
Equipment: blender

Makes 10 portions

1. *Soaking:* Thirty-six to 48 hours before you plan to make the tiramisu, soak Irish moss in cold water to cover then rinse very well. (You should have 1 1/2 oz/45 g of soaked Irish moss.) Set aside.

2. The day before you are going to make the tiramisu, in a small bowl, soak almonds in water to cover for 8 hours. Rinse well. Transfer to a blender and add 2 cups (500 mL) water. Follow Steps 2 though 3 for making Pure Almond Milk (see page 28). Set almond milk aside.

3. In another container, infuse ground espresso in 1/4 cup (60 mL) water for 8 hours. Pour through a coffee filter. Discard coffee grounds and set infusion aside.

4. On the day you are making the tiramisu, in a bowl, soak cashew nuts in water to cover for frosting for 4 hours. Rinse well and set aside.

5. *Cake:* In a bowl, combine all ingredients and 2 tbsp (30 mL) of reserved almond milk (Step 2) and mix to a paste of even consistency.

6. Place mixture in an 8-inch (20 cm) cake pan. Place in freezer and let it set while preparing mocha.

7. *Mocha:* In blender, combine all ingredients including reserved soaked Irish moss. Add reserved coffee infusion and 1/2 cup (125 mL) reserved almond milk and blend to a liquid of even consistency.

8. Remove cake from freezer. Immediately pour mocha on cake. Return cake to freezer to allow it to set.

9. *Frosting:* In blender, combine all ingredients plus reserved soaked cashews. Add 1 cup (250 mL) of reserved almond milk and blend to a creamy liquid of even consistency.

10. Remove cake from freezer and check to ensure that mocha has solidified before putting frosting on cake. Return frosted cake to freezer for about 2 hours to allow it to set.

11. Just before serving, sprinkle with cocoa powder.

TIPS

Keeps 10 days in the refrigerator covered tightly with plastic wrap or for up to 4 months in the freezer.

Date Squares

1	recipe Date Square Crust (see below)	1
1²/₃ cups	whole dried seedless dates	400 mL
²/₃ cup	dried figs, hulled	150 mL
1½ tsp	orange zest	7 mL
½ cup	Date Paste (page 25)	125 mL
2 tbsp	agave nectar	30 mL
1 tsp	alcohol-free vanilla essence	5 mL
⅛ tsp	sea salt	0.5 mL

Preparation: 15 minutes
Equipment: food processor

Makes 8 portions

1. Line a 6- to 8-inch (15 to 20 cm) diameter cake pan with two-thirds of the crust. Set remaining aside.
2. With a knife, coarsely chop dates, figs and orange zest. Place in a bowl. Add remaining ingredients and mix by hand.
3. Add mixture to cake pan over crust, then place remaining crust on top.

TIP

Keeps 10 days in the refrigerator in an airtight container or for up to 4 months in the freezer.

Date Square Crust

²/₃ cup	Brazil nuts	150 mL
¼ cup	macadamia nuts	60 mL
1½ cups	shredded coconut	375 mL
4	seedless dates or ¼ cup (60 mL) Date Paste (page 25)	4
½ tsp	alcohol-free vanilla essence	2 mL
¼ tsp	sea salt	1 mL

Preparation: 5 minutes
Equipment: food processor

Makes 1 crust

1. In food processor, combine Brazil nuts and macadamia nuts and blend to small pieces.
2. Add remaining ingredients and blend to an evenly consistent crust that can be formed into a ball.

TIP

Keeps 2 weeks in the refrigerator in an airtight container.

Dark Chocolate

½ cup	cocoa butter	125 mL
¼ cup	coconut oil	60 mL
¼ cup	agave nectar	60 mL
½ tsp	alcohol-free vanilla essence	2 mL
⅛ tsp	sea salt	0.5 mL
1 cup	packed cocoa powder	250 mL

Preparation: 15 minutes

Equipment: food processor, stove or dehydrator, chocolate molds

Makes about 35 small chocolates (depending on molds)

1. Melt cocoa butter and coconut oil in dehydrator or bain-marie. In bain-marie, stir constantly so that the temperature does not exceed 105°F (41°C).

2. Place melted cocoa butter in food processor. Add remaining ingredients except cocoa powder and blend to obtain a mixture of even consistency.

3. Add half the cocoa powder and blend by pulsing to prevent lumps from forming (not mixed enough) and to prevent chocolate from hardening or solidifying (mixed too much).

4. Add remaining cocoa powder and blend mixture for a few seconds to obtain a silky texture.

5. Pour mixture into molds and refrigerate for 2 hours.

TIPS

For variety, place a pecan, a goji berry or a lemon zest in each hole in the mold.

Keeps 2 weeks in the refrigerator in an airtight container or for up to 4 months in the freezer.

CHOCOLATE

Good news: cocoa abounds in nutrients!

Called Theobroma (the food of the gods) by the Aztecs, cocoa is an excellent source of antioxidants and magnesium. Raw cocoa has a special place in our kitchens!

Cocoa, one of the most popular products of consumption on the planet, has the power to bewitch food lovers and health researchers alike. Indeed, it seems that no one can resist chocolate!

Delving deeper into the subject, we find that cocoa is one of the most chemically complex food substances. Chemical compounds like polyphenols, psychoactive substances like serotonin, antioxidants like catechin, calcium... chocolate has all the qualities of a euphoric drug. Consumed in moderation, it plays a role in maintaining the health of the entire body, especially the heart. It also helps to soothe muscle or menstrual cramps. It's no coincidence that women instinctively crave chocolate during that time in their cycle.

Dark Nougat

1 tbsp	coconut oil, melted	15 mL
1 tbsp	sunflower lecithin	15 mL
1/4 tsp	lemon juice	1 mL
1/4 cup	agave nectar	60 mL
1/4 cup	water	60 mL
1/8 tsp	sea salt	0.5 mL
1/2 cup	cocoa powder	125 mL

For matcha-coated nougats

2 tbsp	matcha powder	30 mL

For coconut-coated nougats

3 tbsp	shredded coconut	45 mL

For ambassador balls

2/3 cup	hazelnuts, reduced to crumbs in food processor	150 mL
1/2	recipe Dark Chocolate, melted (page 209)	1/2

Preparation: 10 minutes
Equipment: blender, stove or dehydrator

Makes 15 nougats

1. In blender, combine all ingredients except cocoa powder and blend to a liquid of even consistency. While blender is running, add cocoa powder and continue to blend until cocoa is incorporated.

2. Pour mixture into a rectangular dish to a depth of 3/4 inches (2 cm). Place in freezer and allow nougats to set for 3 hours.

3. Cut into 15 cubes, place in a container and refrigerate.

4. To coat, roll nougats in a dish of matcha or coconut until they are completely coated.

5. For ambassador balls, roll nougats in hazelnut crumbs until they are completely coated.

6. Pour melted dark chocolate into a bowl. Using a fork, dip balls of coated nougat in chocolate, then place on parchment paper. Refrigerate for 1 hour to allow them to set.

TIP
Keeps 2 weeks in the refrigerator in an airtight container or 2 months in the freezer.

Vanilla Ice Cream

1 cup	cashew nuts	250 mL
$^2/_3$ cup	unpeeled almonds	150 mL
1$^3/_4$ cups	water	425 mL
1 tbsp	soy lecithin	15 mL
$^1/_4$ cup	agave nectar	60 mL
2 tbsp	alcohol-free vanilla essence	30 mL
$^1/_4$ + $^1/_8$ tsp	sea salt	1.5 mL

Soaking: 8 hours
Preparation: 20 minutes
Churning and freezing: according to ice cream maker's instructions
Equipment: blender and ice cream maker

Makes 4 cups (1 L)

1. *Soaking:* In a bowl, soak cashew nuts and almonds in water to cover for 8 hours. Rinse thoroughly and discard soaking water.

2. Make a milk with soaked nuts and water (page 28). (Makes 1$^1/_2$ cups/375 mL cashew-almond milk.)

3. In blender, combine nut milk and remaining ingredients and blend to a creamy liquid.

4. Pour mixture into ice cream maker and start cycle.

5. When ice cream is ready, empty into a container and place in freezer. Good ice cream makers churn and freeze cream at the same time; 30 minutes is sufficient in the freezer to give the cream a firm texture. If the ice cream maker only churns, the ice cream will need to sit in the freezer for several hours to obtain a firm texture

TIP
Keeps 3 months in the freezer.

Soft Banana Cream

4	peeled frozen bananas	4
1 cup	frozen raspberries	250 mL
2 tbsp	agave nectar	30 mL
$^1/_8$ tsp	Himalayan rose salt	0.5 mL

Preparation: 10 minutes
Equipment: blender or juice extractor

Makes 4 cups (1 L)

1. Run frozen fruits through juice extractor or blender to reduce them to a cream.

2. Place cream in a bowl, then incorporate agave nectar and salt.

3. Serve immediately. Do not refreeze, as the cream will crystallize.

Bliss Balls

¼ cup	chopped dried apricots	60 mL
⅓ cup	water	75 mL
2 cups	shredded coconut	500 mL
½ cup	unpeeled almonds	125 mL
½ cup	sultana raisins	125 mL
¼ cup	packed goji berries	60 mL
1 tsp	almond essence	5 mL
1 tsp	orange essence	5 mL
½ tsp	ground cardamom	2 mL
⅛ tsp	sea salt	0.5 mL
¼ cup	Date Paste (page 25)	60 mL
3 tbsp	chia seeds	45 mL

Soaking: at least 15 minutes
Preparation: 20 minutes
Equipment: food processor

Makes 20 balls

1. *Soaking:* In a bowl, soak dried apricots in ⅓ cup (75 mL) water for at least 15 minutes.

2. In food processor, combine all ingredients except apricots, date paste and chia seeds and blend to obtain a sticky mixture. This can take several minutes. Set aside.

3. In food processor, reduce apricots and their soaking water to a purée of even consistency.

4. Pour both mixtures into a bowl, then add date paste and chia seeds. Blend thoroughly to obtain a malleable paste of even consistency.

5. With an ice cream scoop or melon baller, form balls 1 inch (2.5 cm) in diameter. Roll them between the palms of the hand to make very round balls.

TIP

Keeps 1 month in the refrigerator in an airtight container or for up to 4 months in the freezer.

Cocoa Macaroons

½ cup	Brazil nuts	125 mL
2 cups	shredded coconut, divided	500 mL
½ cup	Date Paste (page 25)	125 mL
¼ cup	cocoa powder	60 mL
1 tbsp	agave nectar	15 mL
¼ tsp	alcohol-free vanilla essence	1 mL
⅛ tsp	sea salt	0.5 mL

Preparation: 20 minutes
Equipment: food processor

Makes 20 macaroons

1. In food processor, combine Brazil nuts and half of the shredded coconut and purée to a butter that is as creamy as possible.

2. Add remaining ingredients and blend for a few minutes. Mixture should be of even consistency, but not liquid.

3. Pour mixture into a bowl and incorporate remaining shredded coconut by hand. Knead thoroughly to obtain a black, sticky and very malleable paste.

4. With an ice cream scoop or melon baller, form balls 1 inch (2.5 cm) in diameter. Roll them between the palms of the hand to make very round macaroons.

TIP

Keeps 1 month in the refrigerator in an airtight container or for up to 4 months in the freezer.

Banana Split

1	banana	1
	Pieces of Brownies (see below)	
2	balls of Vanilla Ice Cream (page 213)	2
2 tsp	Macaramel (see right)	10 mL
2 tsp	Raspberry Coulis (page 188)	10 mL
1 tsp	cocoa powder	5 mL
3	mint leaves	3

Preparation: 25 minutes
Equipment: food processor, dehydrator or stove, blender

Makes 1 banana split

1. Cut banana in half lengthwise into 4 pieces, then in half across the width.
2. Lay pieces of banana and brownie in dish, then two balls of ice cream.
3. Pour Macaramel and Raspberry Coulis over all ingredients in dish. Sprinkle cocoa powder over all and garnish with mint leaves. Serve cold.

Brownies

1½ cups	whole seedless dates	375 mL
3 cups	pecans	750 mL
¾ cup	Date Paste (page 25)	175 mL
¾ cup	cocoa powder	175 mL
1½ tsp	alcohol-free vanilla essence	7 mL
⅛ tsp	sea salt	0.5 mL
	Chocolate Frosting (see below)	

1. With a knife, cut dates to make sure they do not contain pits. Next, cut dates coarsely by running them briefly through the food processor. Set aside in a large bowl.
2. Coarsely chop pecans in food processor. Add chopped dates. Incorporate remaining ingredients and blend by hand to a thick paste of even consistency.
3. Spread mixture in an 8-inch (20 cm) square cake pan. Use a spatula to even out mixture. Cut brownie in half lengthwise into 8 pieces, then in half across the width, then on the diagonal.
4. Spread with Chocolate Frosting. Refrigerate for 1 hour to allow frosting to set.

Chocolate Frosting

1 tbsp	water	15 mL
¼ cup	cocoa powder	60 mL
¼ cup	agave nectar	60 mL
½ tsp	alcohol-free vanilla essence	2 mL
⅛ tsp	sea salt	0.5 mL
¼ cup	coconut oil, melted	60 mL

1. In a blender, combine frosting ingredients except coconut oil and blend to a cream of even consistency. Add melted coconut oil and blend until thoroughly incorporated.

TIP

Keeps 2 weeks in the refrigerator in an airtight container or for up to 4 months in the freezer.

Macaramel

¼ cup	macadamia nuts	60 mL
1 tbsp	sunflower lecithin or soy lecithin	15 mL
1 tbsp	maca powder	15 mL
2 tbsp	water	30 mL
¾ cup	agave nectar	175 mL
1 tsp	alcohol-free vanilla essence	5 mL
⅛ tsp	sea salt	0.5 mL

Preparation: 5 minutes
Equipment: blender

Makes 1½ cups (375 mL)

1. In blender, combine all ingredients and blend to a smooth, creamy caramel.

2. Refrigerate for at least 30 minutes for a smooth caramel or 3 hours for a thick, sticky caramel.

TIP
Keeps 3 weeks in the refrigerator in an airtight container.

Cinnamon Buns

Caramel Coulis

1/4 cup	chopped dried apricots	60 mL
1/4 cup	water	60 mL
1/4 cup	Date Paste (page 25)	60 mL
1 1/2 tsp	Ginger Juice (page 24) or 1 tbsp (15 mL) finely grated ginger	7 mL
1 1/2 tsp	freshly squeezed lemon juice	7 mL
1/4 cup	agave nectar	60 mL
1 tsp	sea salt	5 mL

Brioche

1 cup	water	250 mL
1/2 cup	shredded coconut	125 mL
1 cup	unpeeled almonds, chopped in food processor	250 mL
2 cups	ground almonds	500 mL
1/2 cup	ground flax seeds	125 mL
3/4 cup	Date Paste (page 25)	175 mL
2 tsp	alcohol-free vanilla essence	10 mL
1 tbsp	ground cinnamon	15 mL
1 tsp	sea salt	5 mL
1/4 cup	dried currants	60 mL
	Crème Anglaise (see right)	

Soaking: at least 15 minutes
Preparation: 25 minutes
Dehydration: 8 hours
Equipment: food processor, blender, dehydrator, nonstick dehydrator sheet

Makes 16 portions

1. *Caramel Coulis:* Soak dried apricots in 1/4 cup (60 mL) water for at least 15 minutes.

2. In blender, blend apricots and their soaking water with rest of coulis ingredients. Reduce to a sauce. Set aside 1/2 cup (125 mL) of coulis in refrigerator. (It will be used to decorate the cake.)

3. *Brioche:* In blender, make a milk with water and shredded coconut (see Nut Milks, page 21). Set aside 1/2 cup (125 mL) of this milk.

4. In a bowl, by hand, blend half of the chopped almonds with ground almonds, ground flax seeds, date paste, vanilla essence, cinnamon and salt.

5. Gradually add 1/2 cup (125 mL) of coconut milk to this mixture to obtain a sticky paste.

6. Spread paste across entire width of a nonstick dehydrator sheet, but only three-quarters of the length. Spread the rest of the chopped almonds and the currants on this paste. Pour caramel coulis over half of the paste.

7. Roll up paste, starting at the bottom, as you would for a buche de Noël. If needed, use a spatula to lift the paste.

8. Place in dehydrator and dehydrate at 105°F (41°C) for 1 hour. Turn roll over and place on a rack. Let dehydrate again for 1 hour at the same temperature.

9. Cut roll into 16 slices. Lay slices on 2 dehydrator racks and continue to dehydrate at the same temperature for another 6 hours.

10. Serve with Crème Anglaise and decorate with lines of caramel coulis.

TIP

Keeps 2 weeks in the refrigerator in an airtight container.

Crème Anglaise

¼ cup	walnuts	60 mL
¼ cup	Brazil nuts	60 mL
¼ cup	cashew nuts	60 mL
¾ cup	water	175 mL
2 tbsp	agave nectar	30 mL
½ tsp	lemon juice	2 mL
½ tsp	alcohol-free vanilla essence	2 mL
⅛ tsp	ground nutmeg	0.5 mL
⅛ tsp	sea salt	0.5 mL
1 tbsp	coconut oil, melted	15 mL

Preparation: 5 minutes
Equipment: blender

Makes 2 cups (500 mL)

1. Place all ingredients in blender except melted coconut oil and reduce to a smooth cream of even consistency.

2. While blender is running, incorporate melted coconut oil.

3. Let thicken for at least 30 minutes in the refrigerator before serving.

TIP

Keeps 2 weeks in the refrigerator in an airtight container.

Acknowledgments

This book would not have been possible without the help and inspired contributions of many members of Crudessence. We would like to thank the entire team, our faithful customers, who have been asking for this book for several years, and Les Éditions de l'Homme, who dared to venture off the beaten path.

A very special thanks to the following people:

Maxime Lehmann, for writing the recipes in understandable language and for spending more time on the project than we ourselves;

Stéphanie Audet, for her lively representation of our philosophy and for her impressive culinary talent;

Solène Thouin, for having tried all the recipes in the comfort of her home;

Xavier Guérin, for his artistic spontaneity in food styling the dishes;

Marta Menes, for her recipes and her Spanish accent;

Barry Pall, for his straightforwardness, his recipes and his Mexican penchant;

Julian Giacomelli, for his total dedication;

Yanik Karch, Mathieu Rivet, Maya Furuta, Laura Pasichnyk, Chantal Côté, Géraldine Sauvignet, Katharina Pitczuk and Dawn Mauricio, for enlivening the dishes with their personal flair.

Index

Library and Archives Canada Cataloguing in Publication

Côté, David, 1982-
    Rawessence : 180 delicious recipes for raw living / David Côté & Mathieu Gallant.

Translation of: Crudessence.
Includes index.
ISBN 978-0-7788-0446-8

    1. Raw foods. 2. Raw food diet. 3. Vegan cooking. 4. Cookbooks. I. Gallant, Mathieu, 1977- II. Title.

TX837.C6713 2013   641.5'636   C2012-907539-6